# In the garden

**More Books
by
Nancy Wiltgen**


*Bridging Over with Guidance*

*My Heart's Desire—*

*Mine not Yours*

# In the garden

## Through the Narrow Gate

Autobiography by
### NANCY WILTGEN

iUniverse LLC
Bloomington

**In the Garden**
**Through the Narrow Gate**

iUniverse books may be ordered through booksellers or by contacting:

iUniverse LLC
1663 Liberty Drive
Bloomington, IN 47403
www.iuniverse.com
1-800-Authors (1-800-288-4677)

ISBN: 978-1-4759-9642-5 (sc)
ISBN: 978-1-4759-9645-6 (hc)
ISBN: 978-1-4759-9644-9 (ebk)

Library of Congress Control Number: 2013911807

Printed in the United States of America

iUniverse rev. date: 07/15/2013

## About The Author

Because of an encounter with God, Nancy's life changed drastically. All because of a simple prayer calling out to God for help for her child.

She began to have a personal relationship with God and she also was battling Satan at the same time. She had no clue what a spiritual battle was all about!

As she entered into a spiritual journey, she learned to read the Bible and encountered a new group of people called Charismatic Catholics. With her new gifts of visions, speaking in tongues, the gift of prophecy, laying of hands, and hearing God speak to her. With all of these special gifts the Lord blended this new style of living into her life.

As her faith grew stronger she was given the opportunity to travel to Indiana, Missouri, Pennsylvania, and Texas to attend Catholic Charismatic Conferences. She says she has learned a lot of information about being a born again Christian. She would like to invite you to find that personal relationship with God. It is simple, all you have to do is invite the Lord into your heart to be your Lord and Savior and ask that "He" forgives all of your sins. He loves you and He's waiting for that invitation from you.

## *Dedication*

I want to thank the Lord for reaching down and touching my life in an unbelievable way. He opened my mind to the Holy Spirit. I was guided through prayers by a freedom of choice.

The Lord lifted a veil and revealed to me a spiritual walk with him as my loving father.

As the Holy Spirit guided me through my writings, it was revealed to me a pattern that was laid out for me from the beginning of time. I began to witness a linking process that was taking place in my life with all the people around me.

As I watched, my whole life began to take on a whole new way of thinking. I learned to pray and listen for God's voice. I allowed him to use me to help others. Then my life began to take on a completely new meaning.

I thank the lord for my husband, children, grandchildren, and great grandchild, for the family I was born into, and the three sets of spiritual family he gave me.

I would also like to thank all of the priests and nuns that were there for me as I was growing up. I know they made a big impact on my life.

A very special thank you, I wish to extend to a Carmelite monk named Father Short, who the Lord referred to as "Little Monk." For all the prayers, tears and smiles he shared with me on my path of my spiritual journey.

Proverbs 3: 5-6, "Trust in the Lord with all thine heart, and lean not unto thine own understanding. In all thine ways acknowledge him, and he shall direct thy paths."

Matthew 7: 13-14, "Enter ye in at the strait gate: for wide is the gate, and broad is the way, that leadeth to destruction, and may there be which go in thereat: Because strait is the gate, and narrow is the way, which leadeth unto life, and few there be that find it."

Luke 13: 24, "Strive to enter in at the strait gate: for many, I say unto you, will seek to enter in, and shall not be able."

*Editor's Note . . .*

There has been a great debate as to whether or not to capitalize the name "Satan." Since Satan is a name or title, it does go by the grammatical rule of being capitalized. However, many believe that "Satan" should not be capitalized thusly as to not give credit or value to the entity. Satan is the name of the fallen angel who tempts us to sin. Therefore we will capitalize it, while the world continues to debate this topic.

All of the Bible verses used throughout this book are from the Holy Bible, Old King James Version. Feel free to use your favorite version of the Holy Bible as a means of interpretation or comparison.

*Chapter One*

Have you ever wondered if God really exists? Does he really listen to all of our prayers? Does he really care what is happening to us when we are going through bad times and illness?

People in other countries do not have enough food, water, or medicines that they desperately need. There are groups of people marching through areas killing, stealing, raping, and taking what little valuables people may have. Even in our own society, these things are happening.

Many priests, pastors, and evangelists tell us we live in two worlds. They say they occur at the same time. Can it be?

The real world consists of who and what we are and the material things we purchase to show others how important we are, or how rich we can be. Yet this can bring us many problems such as bankruptcy, depression, anxiety attacks, alcoholism, thoughts of suicide, or even turning us to drugs in order to help people deal with their feelings. Many people still feel as if something is missing in their lives.

They also speak about a spiritual world of which not many people like to talk about. Most people are so busy with their lives that they never give it a second thought. Yet, there are thousands of people who go to conferences, seminars, and retreat centers. These people are seeking to hear God's voice. They refer to this as a spiritual journey.

I, myself, had never given it much thought one way or another. Until that day, I was at work praying the rosary. I was working at press number forty-seven. I remember it because it was the same year I was born. As I was assembling the parts, I began to pray for my daughter. She was going through some bad circumstances in her married life. I remember praying that day as I have never done before and to this day, I cannot find words to describe what was happening to me at that time. My prayers that day were very different. Some people say they come from the heart.

I found myself speaking to God as if he were right next to me. I asked God, "Why is this happening to my daughter?" All these bad things were happening to her when she was so far away from me. I told God I felt so helpless! I didn't know what to do about the situation!

Then a thought ran through my mind. I remember thinking, "Have I reached Hell? Why was I thinking that thought?" Then something broke my pattern of thinking. Someone was calling my name. I looked around. I checked with the people who were working around me. Those around me said they had not called me. For safety reasons, we were not allowed to talk while working the presses. I went back to work. Then it happened again. Someone was calling my name . . . Nancy. I felt as if someone was playing a joke on me.

After returning from the restroom, once again, someone was calling my name. As I looked up in shock to what I was seeing with my eyes wide open. There was the Blessed Mother coming towards me. She wore a beautiful blue and white gown. It was then I realized who was calling my name. She was moving freely in my mind, as she was moving closer to me.

After many, difficult struggles here in this world and at the same time the spiritual world, which combined both worlds together as one, the Lord began to speak to me. I learned that I was on a path to a journey of "Enlightenment."

God has taught me that he is everywhere. No matter what direction I turn. I also learned that the Bible can speak to us and that I was an open vessel meaning someone who is open to the Holy Spirit. He has taught me to use my real world to reach out and help others when he leads me to.

The Bible speaks about signs and wonders. How people fasted and prayed for each other. I know God lifted the veil from my eyes. God began to teach me a new direction for my life. I feel like a new creation in God's hands. God truly is the potter and he has remolded my life. He has taught me to walk in this world while keeping my eyes, ears, heart, and mind focused on him. Not the scenario I am going through with all the fears that go through my mind.

My life became a battlefield of good and evil thoughts. Yet, through the knowledge of the Holy Spirit, I drew closer to God every day. I became aware of his presence in my life on a daily basis.

I learned to be in tune to the voice of God as he led me from one experience to another and to learn about many people whose lives were interweaved with mine. God has given me a true meaning in life on how to reach out and guide others.

I have learned that people are at various levels spiritually, but God has taught me that we are links to one another in this world for this is how God created man.

My hope in sharing my story with you is that God will bless you and lift the veil from your eyes. May you enjoy the rewards of a love relationship with our heavenly Father.

As I began to write my story, the Lord led me back to the time I was in my mother's womb and he began to unfold the hidden mysteries of my life. The signs were there all the time. I just did not know it.

My attachment to Mary was in God's plan for me. If it had not been for her, I might not have found my way to Jesus, her son. Yet, in God's timing, he reached out to me and in a step of faith, I moved forward. Through the Holy Spirit, as a gift, I received a completely new prayer life, which was previously unknown to me it is called praying in tongues. This kind of prayer reaches all the way back to the life of Christ. Through a twist of events, I began to understand the gifts of discernment, prophesy, visions, laying of hands, gift of tongues, signs, and wonders. However, the most important thing revealed to me was that I must obey God rather than man. I must admit this can be very difficult at times, but he knows what is best for me.

It is my choice to follow him and allow him into my life as I ask for forgiveness for all of my sins. I have found my answer, "Yes, God really does exist!"

Acts 7: 48-50, "Howbeit the most High dwelleth not in temples made with hands; as saith the prophet, Heaven is my throne, and earth is my footstool: what house will ye build me? Saith the Lord: or what is the place of my rest? Hath not my hand made all these things?"

*Chapter Two*

August 5, 2003

A few months ago, I received a card and on it was written: What if the different roads we traveled before we met had never come together?

Many people feel that life just happens and others see a line of coincidences when things just seem to fall in order. As for myself, I never gave it much thought one way or another. I did not realize it at the time it was occurring, but God was working in me. He had a mighty plan for my life.

I remember hearing stories about my birth. I nearly died from having a bleeding bowel. I received a blood transfusion right after birth and as a precautionary measure, the nuns at St. Joseph's hospital baptized me. It was February 4, 1947. I was one of the first babies that Dr. Bush delivered during the early years of his practice.

I was baptized once again in Holy Angels Catholic Church on February 23, 1947 with my grandparents as my sponsors. I was baptized Anna Caroline Genevieve. Back in those times, they used your saints' names when they baptized a baby.

My parents married on May 4, 1946. Each of them came from a large family. Both families each had six children. My dad had two brothers and three sisters. This consisted of one set of twins that were not identical. My dad was the second from the eldest. His family lived on a small farm.

As for my mother, she had five sisters. One had died as an infant. Mom was the second from the youngest. Contrary to my dad, she grew up in a small city atmosphere.

After their marriage, they built a small house just down the road from my dad's parents. It was near a place called Five Corners.

Our home was small. We had an outside toilet and a green water pump. We carried our water into the house by bucket. We used an oil burner stove to keep the house warm in the winter. Our garden was large and grew mostly potatoes. Eventually, our home held seven people with me being the eldest of five children.

The house sat in a quiet setting with pastures all around us. There were two ponds, but we play in one, as the other was too deep. In the summer, we went to catch frogs and pick wild flowers. In the winter despite the cold Wisconsin temperatures, we would go sleigh riding. Down the hills and sometimes across the frozen pond, we would slide for hours.

My grandfather was still plowing his land with horses and old-fashioned farm equipment while our neighbors used tractors. From what I understood, he was the last farmer in the country to farm in this manner.

I do not remember much of my early years, at least not until about first grade. My most outstanding memory was my first Holy Communion. All dressed in white, with a veil, right down to long white stocking and white shoes. I received my first communion on May 15, 1955, at Holy Trinity Church. The church was beautifully decorated with flowers. However, the ones I remember were the lilacs. There were three colors of lilacs, light purple, dark purple, and white.

The nun played an old-fashioned pump organ as we marched down the center aisle. I remember carrying my new rosary. It was white with gold trim. I also carried my new prayer book. The cover resembled marble. The cover read "First Steps to Jesus." There was a picture of a host and chalice on the cover.

Back at that time, all the drinking fountains were covered with a large piece of white cloth. No food or liquid was allowed before receiving communion. After a few weeks, I developed a problem whenever I did my fasting before mass. I felt like I wanted to faint. The nun came and asked me why I was not participating in communion and explained to me the importance of uniting with Jesus. I explained to her and the next thing I knew I was excused from class to take a walk over to the priest's house to have a talk with him. I was so excited because after our talk, I was given special permission to have water or juice one hour before communion. I never had a problem after that.

My school was built right next door to the church. This is where I attended my first eight years of schooling. The building itself was very old. On the walls near the front door hung pictures of previous graduating classes, including a picture of my twin aunts who graduated the year I was born. Above the school was a convent where the nuns lived. There were always good smells of homemade bread and soups drifting downstairs. I remember one nun who would collect rose pedals. She would grind them up and made homemade rose smelling beads that she formed into rosaries that were sold to help raise money. On rainy or very cold days, when there were blizzards, we would march through an underground tunnel, which linked the school and convent to the church.

My closest friend was Mary Ann. We played on the playground, which consisted of swings made with wooden seats. There was a merry-go-round, a teeter-totter, and a baseball field. Every day started the same way with mass. We would pick a partner and march over to the church in silence.

Looking back, I realized that this church played an important part in my life. There were a lot of old fashion statues there, but the most important one to me was the statue of Mary, our Blessed Mother. I do believe this stems from the teachings I had received from the nuns. Mary represented our earthly mother, someone you could pray to and talk to whenever you had a problem in life. The months of May and October were set aside especially for praying the rosary.

I remember being taught in school that each home was to have a May alter. So of course, I had my small statue of Mary with a small jar of wild yellow dandelions and set them on the table in my bedroom. This is where the family was supposed to pray together.

Each year at graduation time, a name of a graduating girl was randomly selected for a special honor. The one chosen had the honor of crowning the statue of Mary. She was given the honor of wearing a bride's dress. One small girl was selected from the first communion class to carry in the ring of flowers, which was placed on the statue during the service.

In the church near the front alter high upon a pedestal, stands another statue of Mary. I can remember many times I would visit the church after school. All the kids would go home and the nuns would go upstairs. I was alone waiting for my dad to pick me up after work. The only other person I would see was the janitor. He never spoke except to say hello.

I would sneak into the empty church, sit in the front row, and stare at Mary high on her pedestal. There I would talk to Mary about all my problems. I would sit for a long time staring at this statue's lips, waiting for her to speak to me. However, she never did. Yet, I would always return for another visit.

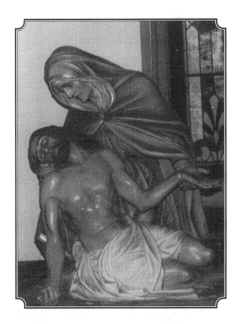

There was another statue of Mary in our church. She was holding Jesus in her arms after he was taken down from the cross. This statue is named the Pieta`. The Pieta` sits in the back corner of the church. Each time I left the building, I would talk to Mary. Still there was no answer. In front of the statue was a kneeler. I would stand on it and stretch up on my toes so I could reach the nail hole in Jesus' hand. I would kiss the nail hole in Jesus's extended hand. I would then say the verse the nuns had taught us. Luke 23:34, "Then said Jesus, Father, forgive them; for they know not what they do . . ."

Once again, there was no answer, but the small child that I was would return each day to talk with Mary. As I grew older, I realized no answer was coming my way.

Growing older, I learned more about praying the rosary and the lighting of candles to represent us being present in church even if we were not there. Most important, someone gave me a small book that had the novena prayers, which I recited for nine days. The prayers were to Saint Ann, the mother of Mary. I used this book even into my adult life.

As the years passed by into my eighth year of school, I headed for confirmation. The nuns drilled us as we memorized our catechism questions.

One question that sticks in my mind is, "Where is God?" God is everywhere!

This was a big occasion in our life as we were able to pick a name of our choice to be added to our baptismal name. I chose the name Elizabeth after my great-grandmother. It also was my great aunt's name, whom I chose to be my sponsor. We share the same birthday. My sister who was in the seventh grade was also confirmed that day. She took the name Frances after our other great-grandmother.

Since this was a big event in our lives, we were allowed to wear new clothes. My sister was given a beautiful new blue and white dress with an artificial flower. I was given a bright yellow satin dress. It was my cousin's prom dress, which needed to be hemmed. The seamstress added a white turn down collar and an artificial flower.

So there I stood with my newly permed, overly tight, cut way too short, red curly hair in a bright yellow satin dress. To top it off, we had to wear a white gown with a red collar and a red hat with a white beanie on top. I took one look at myself in the mirror and I wanted to cry. I hated the way I looked. However, most important, I tried to keep my mind on all the questions I had memorized. Luckily, I was never called on. It finally came time for the Archbishop to anoint us with oil, lay hands on us, and pray for the "Gifts of the Holy Spirit." As he prayed over me, I was surprised as he read off my names Anna Caroline Genevieve Elizabeth Mary.

Wow! Five names were recited. My aunt gave me a beautiful rosary that day, which I still have today. Over the years, it has broken and been mended several times. I also have a picture of my confirmation class. I am in the top row, my head tipped back and my eyes are looking upward.

Lord only knows what I was thinking at the time.

# *Chapter Three*

I
t was a great summer that year. Mary Ann's dad picked up my sister and I nearly every other day. We went out in the fields and picked little green pickles for the cannery. I think I earned a grand total of about seven dollars. That was a lot of money for me. I purchased my Saint Pius, the ten daily missal.

Finally, the big day arrived on May 21, 1961. I wore a beautiful blue lace dress. Once again, a picture of our class was added to the wall with the pictures of the previous graduates.

As for my religious training, I was expected to attend classes once a week. It consisted of a workbook and movies. The priest would give lectures on different subjects. I vaguely remember the priest talking about the changes in the church. It was something called Vatican II. From my point of view, it was not a top priority in my life at the time.

When I entered high school, I lost my best friend. Her family lived in another school district. The Lord did not waste any time giving me new friends. The day I went to register for my freshman year, I went with my friend Patty. We had known each other since we were five years old. It was she who introduced me to a new girl named Catherine. She was in need of a few dollars to purchase a ticket so she could attend the sporting events at the high school during the coming year. My parents were upset that I would lend money to a total stranger. To my delight, she was in my homeroom. Her locker was only a few doors away from mine. I remember thanking God for this new friendship because I was separated from all of my old classmates. I did have the opportunity to see a few of my old classmates on the bus and sometimes to say hello to them during lunchtime.

My life in high school was a difficult struggle for me. I had average grades and my eyesight had been bad since the first grade. After having a physical exam upon entering high school, it was determined that I had to have glasses. I can still remember the first time I saw leaves on a tree. From a distance, it overwhelmed me. From that time on, I never wanted to remove the glasses from my face.

Not being able to see very well affected my learning abilities. It was difficult for me to see the black board when the nuns were teaching. Coming from a small town, there were other problems for me to tackle. The other kids who had been in public school were more advanced in their studies. They even had gym class!

Now I was challenged with my first gym class during my freshman year. As we all gathered together on that first day to meet the teacher, I saw one girl sitting alone. Her name was also Nancy and we became best friends. She was raised on a farm. She did not wear fancy clothes or lots of make-up. The one thing that we both loved to do was to fix our hair. Back in the sixties, this was extremely important. It was the time for Elvis, the Beatles, Chubby Checker, Rock and Roll music, boyfriends, playing baseball and babysitting.

During my sophomore year of high school, I had my appendix removed and suffered from stomach ulcers. I began to date the man I eventually married. This was also the year when my parents purchased a different house. To my surprise, Catherine lived down the road from us.

June 10, 1965, while dressed in a red robe, I marched down the aisle and received my high school diploma.

Thinking back through those four years of my life, I definitely feel I had put Jesus in the back seat of my life. Even though I attended my religion classes, and went to Sunday mass, my connection to prayer had slipped away.

*Chapter Four*

One month after graduation on July 10, 1965, I was married in Holy Trinity Church. About two weeks before the wedding a new law was passed in the church. It allowed Catholics who married someone not of the same faith the opportunity to say their wedding vows at the communion rail. Before that time, people were married in the priest's house.

Getting things together seemed stressful as I guess everyone has that problem but everything fell in order. Thank God. The selection of a wedding dress turned into a problem. Someone purchased an old prom dress for me. As I looked at the dress, the words of the priest ran through my mind. For he cautioned me, "Make sure that your dress covers your body or I will not marry you in the church."

As I looked at this strapless yellowing prom dress, I began to cry and pray. Later on I found out that the dress had come from a thrift shop. I took the dress back and on the counter was a sign that said no returns. I spoke to an elderly lady and explained my situation. She called to a man working in another room. She asked him if he had unpacked a load of boxes that had arrived the day before. He told her that he unpacked just a few of the boxes.

She excused herself and in a few minutes, she returned carrying a long white gown with long sleeves. It seemed like a miracle.

She told me that a local bridal shop went out of business and had donated several dresses. This dress was the only one close to my size.

With a big smile on her face, she handed me the dress and told me it was an even exchange.

The dress was exactly my size!

I borrowed a veil from Nancy's sister. The flowers I carried were white carnations with one large lavender orchid in the center.

Catherine's mom sewed the bridesmaids' dresses. They wore white dresses; one trimmed in a light green and the other a pale orchid. The bridesmaids carried a bouquet of flowers consisting of daisies and mums.

After our wedding vows were spoken, the witnesses were taken aside to sign the wedding documents. At that time a man whom I had baby-sat for his five children, sang the song, "Ave Maria." While he sang, I carried a bouquet of white flowers over to the statue of Mary and laid them on the communion rail in front of her. I stopped for a moment and said a prayer.

## Chapter Five

After a honeymoon to the west coast, we moved into a one bedroom rented house on Alder Street. Below us lived two elderly ladies who were sisters. I had become pregnant with our first child and we accumulated a new landlord. Then we made the decision to move to a larger home with two bedrooms.

Our son was born ten months later on May 12, 1966. Fifteen months later a daughter was born on August 20, 1967. Then about two years later, I had a miscarriage. The doctor informed me that he thought I had been carrying twins.

That is when I went through a period of my life where I hated God. I could not understand why he would allow something like this to happen to me.

Then once again, I became pregnant. The morning sickness grew worse with each pregnancy. What was a minor problem in my other pregnancies was now a major problem. I had blood clots in my right leg from my ankle, all the way to the groin area of my body. The doctor gave me orders to have complete bed rest for nearly seven months. Once again, I turned back to my rosaries and novena prayers. I was drawing closer to God again. Then on March 1, 1970, I gave birth to another baby girl.

Then we moved into our first home which we built from scratch. It was located on Maple Road. It was a small house surrounded with trees we had planted and also had a large garden. We had a swing set and a sandbox.

Right when I thought everything was right in my life, life became a struggle again. With three small children, living out in the country, no driver's license, and my husband began working the night shift. I was separated from family and friends. Even though I spent time working as a volunteer at the school and became a rifle instructor, I still felt an empty feeling in my life. As time moved on more and more problems began to surface in my everyday life.

Then the decision was made. We decided to sell our beautiful white house with olive green trim. We held rummage sales and had an auction. We sold just about everything we owned.

# Chapter Six

We purchased a twenty-seven foot yellow Mallard travel trailer. This became our home. We moved from Wisconsin to Oregon. About a year later, we finally purchased a house across the street from a Catholic school on Ivy Street.

Once again, the Lord gave me a new friend. Her name was also Nancy. She was a retired teacher with two adopted children. We lived next door to a young couple who had just gotten married. I also met a beautiful lady named Mary. She was a teacher from New York City. We lived only a few blocks from the church and once again, I felt drawn closer to God. I did some babysitting for two couples' children. Later I discovered that both couples were ex-priests who were married to ex-nuns. I felt God had put us together.

Once again, there were problems at the plywood mill where my husband worked. The mill was closing down. The wages were low and no jobs to be found. There were even problems in the school system. It seemed like God was closing all the doors on us. Once again, we decided to move on.

*Chapter Seven*

Then we ventured on to Arizona where my sister lived. We eventually purchased a home with lots of bedrooms for everyone. Time moved swiftly during those years and before we knew it, the kids were graduating from high school. All of them had made the honor roll. Each of them was offered scholarships to further their education. Our son graduated from Maryvale High School and the two daughters from Independence High School.

As for my prayer time through the high school years of my children it seemed like a constant time with God. There were prayers for school exams, picking the right friends, illnesses and of course, the everyday problems we had encountered. Things always fell in order but I had never acknowledged the gift coming from God.

Our son purchased the house next door. Our eldest daughter married a man who had just entered the military and our youngest had begun taking classes at the local community college. It seemed for the first time in my life that I had time for myself. I was enjoying the time with my youngest child. Time began to pick up speed and before we knew it, we were grandparents. A baby boy was born on September 17, 1989. Our daughter had complications during his birth. The baby was delivered by a cesarean section. After the delivery of the baby, she developed a life-threatening situation. She had blood clots in her left leg. However, this time I called everyone I knew and asked them for prayers. As time passed, her health improved. She told me that the doctors told her it was an inherited medical problem. She was experiencing additional financial problems as well as other problems that seemed to complicate her life. Besides many prayers, I would send her money and care packages when needed. Occasionally, I would send her tickets to come home for her and the baby to visit.

Meanwhile our youngest daughter began dating a young man whom she had known since grade school. There were many nights when he would come over and join us for supper. After supper, they would do their homework. Sometimes they would invite me to go along with them on their dates. One evening as we were going to a family picnic, we were walking down a path when I stumbled and fell. I did not think much of it because there was no blood or cuts. I just felt terribly embarrassed by the whole situation.

# Chapter Eight

About a week later, I began to feel ill and the doctor could not figure out what was wrong with me. Weeks passed by and I seemed to be getting worse. I could see the doctor was struggling for answers for he could not figure out what was wrong with me. The next thing I knew I was rushed off to the emergency room because I began to spit up blood. I was x-rayed and was told that it was just a touch of pneumonia. However, I knew there was something stuck in my throat. I kept clearing it, but it would always come back.

My friend used to call it a "hair ball." I remember being in a lot of pain at night, and it had come to my mind to sit up and put my arms over the top of the sofa with a pillow under my chin. My head was tilted backwards so I could sleep.

Then one morning I awoke to find my face blue in color. The week before, I had made an appointment with a pulmonary specialist, but I was told I had to wait for two weeks before I could get in to see the doctor. Once again, my daughter put me in the car and drove me to the doctor's office. Like the last few weeks, I would just show up and the nurse would put me in a room to wait to see the doctor. The poor doctor just could not figure out what was going on. At one point, I asked him if he thought I might have a goiter problem. He replied no, for he had just operated on a man for that and was sure that was not it. That morning he told me, I needed help now. The nurse scheduled an appointment for me. I had to go off my insurance plan to see a specialist. The appointment was that same day about two in the afternoon.

My daughter drove me to the office. She dropped me off at the door and went to park the car. I took the elevator to the second floor and entered the reception room. I sat down. The nurse brought me paperwork to fill out. Name, social security number, mother's health, I had gotten to the third question and I just could not do it anymore. The nurse was watching me; she asked if there was a problem. I told her I just could not think. She asked if someone was with me.

"Yes, my daughter is parking the car," I replied.

I remember I was having a difficult time breathing and then my head fell forward. The next thing I knew two women had me by the arms and were taking me back to a room but before I entered, we met the doctor and he asked if I ever had a blood-clotting problem.

I said, "Yes with every pregnancy and with a miscarriage."

Before I could speak another word, I was put in a room with an x-ray machine. Within a few minutes, I was taken to a room and put in a paper gown. It seemed like only seconds to me before the doctor entered the room. He was carrying the x-rays in his hand. I remember asking if my daughter had come in yet.

He said, "She's in the waiting room."

The doctor said he had checked over my x-rays and I had water in my right lung.

He said, "I'm so sorry. I'm going to have to drain your lung right here. It's too dangerous for you to go over to the hospital."

My thoughts were racing through my mind. After all, we were only across the street from Maryvale Hospital. He apologized several more times, as he quickly cut and inserted a tube into my back. He said I should let him know when I felt movement in my lung. There was no time for any kind of drugs to be used to numb the pain as the doctor worked in silence.

To my surprise, I was feeling no pain at all. As I sat on a chair, I was bent over a pillow that was lying on a table in front of me. I remember I was in constant prayer as the doctor was draining my lung.

When he was finished, I dressed. He came back into the room.

He said, "I want to show you what I took out of your lung."

In his hands, he held a medium size bag. It was full of water that had a reddish color to it.

As he smiled at me he asked, "Do you know what's in this bag?"

My reply was no. In fact, I was surprised that anyone could even drain water through a tube out of one's body.

After the procedure he said, "You are very lucky to be alive. Some people have drowned with as little as two teaspoons of water in their lungs. The fluid should be a clear liquid, but yours is full of small blood clots."

As I sat looking at the bag of water, I did not fully comprehend what the doctor was telling me.

Within a few minutes, he was writing out some forms for the hospital with explicit directions.

Then he turned in my direction and asked, "You can take a day or two off can't you? I need to run a few tests."

"Yes, I think I can."

Then he asked my daughter to drive me over to the hospital.

I heard him say, "They'll be waiting for you."

As I got up to leave I reached for my purse.

The doctor asked, "Are you feeling weak? Do you need some help?"

"No," I replied, "I'm fine."

We drove across the street to the hospital. There, a nice hospital volunteer, pushing a wheelchair, met us. She wanted me to sit in it, but I recall telling her I really did not need it, I was feeling fine. After all my color was back to normal, I could breathe without any problems. Then I was told I would have to spend the night and the doctor ordered a series of tests to be done immediately. The nurse gave me a room number then put the ID bracelet on my arm. As I lifted myself up out of the chair, I began to feel weak. The phone was ringing. The doctor was checking to see if I had arrived. I glanced over in the direction of my daughter and told her I think I am ready for the wheel chair now.

*Chapter Nine*

Within minutes, I was assigned a room and was wheeled off for a battery of tests. People were complaining because they had to stay late to perform the tests. The bad part was I was passing all the tests. Somewhere along the line, I was given and IV, which contained a high dosage of blood thinners. The next thing I knew I was meeting a new doctor a woman hematologist. A sense of panic went through me, here stood two specialists who were not on my insurance plan, plus they were telling me that I had to stay in the hospital for at least ten days. After a lot of tests the doctors found a blood clot in my right leg. It began at the ankle and extended up to about one inch below my knee. They said the clots were breaking loose and moving into my right lung.

They decided it must have happened when I had fallen about a month earlier. But I had no pain in my leg that would have indicated that my life was in danger.

After the ten day stay in the hospital, the doctors put me on Coumadin. My diet was restricted from eating green vegetables, my favorite of course! The dietician told me it was a gift from God because they are natural blood thickening foods.

I was told I needed complete bed rest. I found that by taking the Coumadin I was losing my memory. Fear was my consent battle. I was not allowed any privacy. Even taking a shower or simply going to the bathroom by myself was out of the question. The door was left open in case I should fall or hurt myself.

I will never forget the day I was released from the hospital. The doctor walked in and sat on the bed next to me. He began to explain my medications and he was telling me that I would no longer be seeing him. I would return to my family physician. He said that he had another patient like me, except it was a man. He told me that I should have died and that there must be a good reason why I was still here.

I returned to my family doctor to be released to go back to work, but while I was there, I mentioned to him that I felt a small lump under my left jaw. He examined it and decided it could be removed in the office. A few days later, the doctor surgically removed the small non-cancerous tumor.

I went back to work. I felt like I had gone through a battle. I still had this emptiness in my life. Looking back to that time, a wonderful thing had happened to me for some unknown reason my cravings for salt had disappeared. I found myself praying out of frustration more than anything else.

## Chapter Ten

For the next couple of years it seemed like I was searching for the important reason. Why did God leave me here?

Life again fell into a routine. After my youngest daughter was married, she needed to stay here at home because her husband went off to boot camp. She had pretty well decided that I should get my driver's license.

My first thought was, "Yes! I'll have some freedom to come and go as I want."

As I began to study the manual, fear set in after all I was in my late forties now. All the "what ifs" went through my mind; I was facing another kind of problem. My husband did not want me to purchase a car of my own. I did not know what to do. Once again I prayed for directions. Through a twist of fate, once again things fell in order.

I went to the credit union and spoke to a lady there to apply for a loan in just my name. The woman was very compassionate of my problem, because I had never done anything like purchasing a car on my own. She told me step-by-step how to do things. I went to the dealership, picked out the car, and saved enough money for the down payment. Once again, I felt like I was fighting a battle every minute just to buy this car.

Finally, after a few days, the credit union called to let me know that the papers were approved in my name only. I was given the instructions on what to do at the dealership. My daughter and I went in and completed all of the required paperwork. I ordered a green Saturn.

Next I went in and passed my driver's test and everything was falling in place . . . except for one small flaw.

The delivery date was postponed. Another two weeks I was told. I began to worry, since my daughter was scheduled to leave soon. She and her husband were moving to a military base in Oklahoma. I wanted her to help me learn how to handle my new car. For all of my driving lessons was done using her car.

Once again, the car was delayed. This time when I spoke to Mr. Rodriguez, he said, "Didn't anyone tell you they are doing a new color change? This means they have to shut down the lines and change over to the new color that is coming out this year."

My wait continued for another week. Meanwhile, my supervisor informed me that my name came up for a parking space.

She said, "I know you don't drive, but I have to offer it to you because of your seniority." Since the two of us were friends, I confided in her about what I had been doing for the last several months. She agreed to hold the parking spot for me. Thank God.

As time passed, my youngest daughter had to leave to join her husband out of state. About two weeks later, the Saturn dealership called to inform me that the car arrived.

"It came in by train and it was the first one delivered into Phoenix with the new color," the sales representative said.

I was so excited! I took my son with me to pick it up.

The sales representative said, "It's going to be a few minutes wait, because we are washing the car and putting gas into the tank."

Finally, he handed me the keys. I was so very excited!

"It's parked right out front," he said.

So with keys in hand, I went looking for my new car. Where is it? I only had one problem . . . I could not find a green car! I had completely forgotten about the new color. In fact no one ever told me what the new color was. I went back inside.

"What's wrong?"

I replied, "I can't find my car."

Looking out the window, he pointed to one.

"Why that's it right there."

I knew he could see the disappointment on my face.

He quickly added, "I'll tell you what. You can drive this car for the next thirty days. If you are not completely satisfied, you can pick out another car off the lot for an even trade."

With half of a smile, I asked, "What color is that?"

He replied, "Why, it's teal."

# Chapter Eleven

My son was the first person to drive my new car. We took it across the street. Finally, I got behind the wheel. It was very different driving this car. It seemed a lot lower to the ground and the hood was sloped downward.

He looked at me and smiled. Then he said, "Just look straight ahead and drive."

That's just what I did. After about twenty minutes, I felt comfortable with the car. The real shocker came the following morning. I was so excited to show everyone my new car and I even decided to leave very early just in case I would have any trouble parking.

As I opened the front door, it hit me! It was black as midnight. When I was taking my driving lessons, we did very little night driving. For I knew I would not be running around by myself at night.

Now it was the month of October and the sun did not rise until later in the morning. I put my tool bag and my lunch in the car. Then I marched myself right back into the house and called my daughter in Oklahoma.

When she answered, I told her, "Its black as night out there!"

Her reply was, "Oh, my God!"

We had overlooked the fact that fall was here and it would still be dark in the mornings when I left for work. After a few tears and many prayers, I drove myself to the factory. I made it in one piece. I took a deep breath as I pulled into my parking space under a tree that was close to a footbridge.

After a few days, I began to feel quite comfortable driving even in the dark. About a week later, a friend of mine had a flat tire. I stayed after with her and we talked until the wrecker came. Her car had to be towed to the garage.

After the car was hooked up, she asked, "Would you mind driving me to the garage? I don't feel comfortable riding in the truck with some man I don't even know."

Since Bessie and I ate lunch together for years, I felt the need to help her. As we were putting on our seatbelts, I asked for directions.

She said, "It's not far from here. Just down the way on Indian School Road."

So we followed the wrecker and while I was driving, I kept having this thought run through my mind. Before leaving for Oklahoma, my daughter said, "Drive wherever you want to, but please stay off of Indian School Road. It's very dangerous to travel that road."

I arrived home several hours later and the phone was ringing off the hook.

"Hello?"

"Where have you been?" It was my daughter!

Everything was going great. About two weeks later, my husband and I went in to the dealership and purchased an extended warranty for the car. We were given two free t-shirts from the dealership. I even grew accustomed to the color of the car. It was very easy to spot the teal color in the parking lots.

Time flew by. I was enjoying my new life. Sometimes I would go shopping for Christmas gifts or pick up groceries on the way home. I was enjoying a freedom I had never experienced before.

## Chapter Twelve

On May tenth, everyone was looking forward to seeing the solar eclipse. Radio and television reports warned everyone about taking the proper precautions when observing the eclipse.

I remember the day so vividly as if it were yesterday. The table where I was working was very close to a large window in my factory. I remember it was getting very dark outside even though it was the middle of the day. When break time came, I went outside. I saw a friend of mine who worked from the production control office standing outside. She was observing the eclipse with one of our company's engineers. He had designed a special pair of glasses just for the event.

After he was finished, he handed the glasses to her. When she took them off, she asked if I would like to see the eclipse. I was excited I had never seen anything like this. It was remarkable as I looked at the moon and the sun as they had lined up together. For some strange reason, which I did not understand, I saw a quick flickering of movement as I watched. The engineer had another pair of glasses on and I asked him if he had observed the same movement that I had seen.

"No," he replied.

I thanked him for the use of the glasses and excused myself as it was time to go back to work.

It was about that time when my kids began to call home for Mother's Day and share stories about what was going on in their lives. My daughter in Oklahoma always had stories about the bad weather, because of all the tornados that would pass through the area.

My daughter, in Maine, would share stories about how her life was falling apart. I was always glad to hear that she kept herself busy helping the Chaplains on the military base. I knew she was going through some bad circumstances, so once again, I began to pray for them. Then while working the next day at press number forty-seven, I remember it because it was the same year that I was born. I was assembling and pressing the parts and as usual, I began to pray the rosary to help pass the time as I worked. Thoughts of my daughter passed through my mind and I began to pray like I have never done before and to this day I cannot find words to describe what was happening to me at that time. Then for some reason I began to mentally talk to the Lord. Some people refer to this as praying from the heart. I asked God why this was happening to my daughter. All these bad things were happening to her when she was so far away from me. I told God I felt so helpless! I did not know what to do about the situation!

Then I heard a voice say, "Please God take some of this abuse out of my life."

As I listened to my next thought, I heard, "Have I reached Hell?"

As I sat there, I tried to gather my thoughts. I was trying to figure out where these thoughts were coming from. Then something broke my pattern of thinking as I looked around for someone was calling my name. I check with the people who were working around me, but everyone said it was not them. While running our presses it was not out of the ordinary not to talk to each other for safety reasons. Each time I went back to work, it was repeated. I still heard someone audibly calling my name, "Nancy."

As I continued my task, I heard a voice say, "Listen to me, Nancy."

I got up and left the floor to go to the restroom. There I put cool water on my face and then returned to work. This happened to me a few times, as I repeated the steps to the ladies' room.

Then a startling thing happened to me as I looked up from my press with my eyes wide open. I seemed to be looking into another dimension and I could see an image of the Blessed Virgin Mary coming towards me. I began to realize that the audible voice I was hearing was coming from her.

The image I was seeing was in color. She wore a blue and white gown. She kept saying, "Listen to me." I quickly got up from my chair and again went to the restroom. Again, I put some water on my face. Then once again, I went back to the press. This time I sat still as the image came towards me. I felt trapped! I could not get this picture out of my head as it moved about freely in my mind. I could not wait until it was time to go home.

At the same time, I was very fearful. Who could I tell this story to? Who would believe this could happen to anyone? After all, I could not believe it myself.

My drive home was quiet. When I entered the house, I began to hear voices speaking to me. I knew they were not my thoughts, as they seemed separated from my mind. I could sit and listen to conversations that were speaking to me. I decided I would get a paper and pencil and write down what I was hearing.

As I began to focus on what was being said, I came to realize that one voice seemed to be a soft feminine voice. With words of encouragement, that she would take care of me. The voice urged me to pray for the children. Then I began to notice that I was hearing a second voice. It used obscene language. I knew it was not coming from me. I never spoke like that even when I was mad; I never used that kind of language.

I tried to drown out the voices by turning on every electrical appliance in the house. The voices continued. I went to bed early that night only to find out the next day was a repeat. Only now, I realized it was no longer audible but it was my thought waves speaking to me. The colored visions were continuing. I watched Mary float closer to me. I was surprised as I felt a peace come over me.

I could not figure out what was happening to me. Then it came to me. My last child just moved out; perhaps I was suffering from the empty nest syndrome. On the other hand, was it because I was forty-seven years old and that I must be going through menopause? Maybe I was having a mental break down. Boy, I was good at diagnosing myself. I had never heard of someone having a religious encounter like what was happening to me. I do not remember sleeping very much during that time, but life continued just as before.

When I think back to those days I wonder how did I hold myself together going through unbelievable circumstances, as I did then. I came to realize that God was with me and carried me all the way.

Here I was crying out and struggling for help and no one to turn to except God. As I listened to the voices speaking, I learned to rely on the soft-spoken voice, which seemed to give me good directions. I finally had to admit there was someone or something that was stronger than me and that I learned it was coming from God. I learned I was no longer in control but I was learning to give God the control over me by my choice. I was allowing God to make the changes for me.

What was so remarkable was all the circumstances in my life were changing to fit my new lifestyle. It was something I could not explain but like a small child I clung to a voice I knew was Mary, the mother of Jesus.

It was through her voice that I decided to seek help. Mary encouraged me to go and talk to a neighbor who lived just down the street from us. Her husband was a postal employee and for years, our children attended the same schools. We never really visited with each other only to wave as she went off to work each day dressed in a white nurse's uniform.

So once again, I prayed and took a deep breath and walked down the street to have a conversation with a total stranger!

She greeted me with a big smile and welcomed me into her home. I felt very comfortable with her and I began to share with her the strange events that were happening to me. Her response was calm as she began to tell me that she was not raised Catholic; she had changed religions when she married her husband. Now their whole family was Catholic. She shared with me that she grew up in a very small community in one of the southern states. She said when she was a little girl (I believe she said it was her grandmother) had an inoperable tumor near the brain. Someone in the family took her to a tent revival. She said the people there laid hands on her and the tumor totally disappeared! Coming from Wisconsin, I had no clue as to what this woman was even talking about. I remember asking her, "What the heck is a tent revival?" Then she went on to explain that it was a group of people that traveled from town to town and put up a big tent along the side of the road. The preacher would read from the Bible, then they would sing songs and lay hands on the sick people and miracles would happen. She said that after her grandmother was healed, she would still continue going to these revivals and she would get up and give her testimony on what God had done for her.

Then she told me that I was fine and that I was not having a mental breakdown. I was not to worry because God was taking care of me. After our visit, I walked home with a reassurance from a total stranger that I was not to fear the events that were taking place. Because she was a nurse, I felt confidence in the words she had said to me.

Each time the voices continued to speak to me, I would remember what the neighbor lady had told me and then I would feel peace and calmness would come over me.

*Chapter Thirteen*

As time passed, I continued to go through many spiritual chains of events. I still could not figure out what was happening or why this was happening to me.

Then several weeks later on a Saturday morning, I was doing my dishes and cleaning the kitchen. The radio was playing, the dog was sleeping, and my husband went off to take a shower. Sometime later, he came into the kitchen and told me something and to this day I cannot remember what is was, but I was stunned at his comments for he had given me a message of some kind.

I just stood looking at him and asked who told you to tell me that? After all, were all alone in the house.

He had a shocked look on his face and replied, "I don't know. Give me a minute."

Then he turned and walked down the hall to the bathroom. A few minutes later, he returned and sat down at the kitchen table. With tears in his eyes, he told me while he was in the shower Mary spoke with him. She had given him a message for me. Boy, talk about confusion, here was someone not even Catholic hearing from Mary. Then I thought that maybe breakdowns are contagious. Then another thought ran through my brain, what if he was the same as me? I fell apart at that point and began to tell him of all my experiences over the last six weeks. He shared with me a story of a spiritual nature he went through while in high school. Where he felt he had died but came back. It was just a one-time episode. At last, I was free to talk about the things that were happening to me.

# *Chapter Fourteen*

A few days later, I was getting ready to go to work and my thoughts kept telling me that I was going to die that day. I did not want to go to work. I did not want to drive. I told my husband what was going on.

He said, "Just don't believe it; it's not true."

I was crying as I backed my car out of the driveway. I decided to drive very slowly and with a lot of caution. I had made it to the main intersection of Sixty-Seventh Avenue and Camelback. As I approached the intersection, I applied my brakes as the light flashed to yellow. I remember looking up through my rear-view mirror. I saw a "Z twenty-eight" speeding up behind me. I remember watching him swerve around me nearly hitting my car. He continued to drive right through the intersection on a red light. I saw all the lanes were full of cars. Every car had come to a full stop. As I watched him drive through the intersection, I called out to God to help this man, and then I noticed that there were no sounds; just dead silence. Just as I finished thinking that thought, I began to hear birds singing and a lot of horns blowing and people yelling. There was no accident. My mind flashed back to a time when one of my daughters had gone through a similar scenario, only her car was totaled. She had to be cut out of her seatbelt and they pulled her out through the window of her car.

I felt very shaken at what had just happened but I was still alive. I walked into the factory, clocked in, and went to work. The morning's events kept replaying itself in my mind. I told my supervisor I need to go and see my doctor. His office was only a few blocks away. After speaking to him, he said he knew a good psychiatrist he could recommend. After he left the room, I sat for a few minutes and it was at that point I decided that God was going to have to take care of me. I left the office without the referral and went back to work.

Then I decided to share my story with my friend. She was very upset and basically told me some people are more . . . nuts than others. Mary's voice continued to give me confidence, that I was all right and not to worry. She told me that someone else would come and help me.

Within a short time my friend was moved into another department. I was given a new supervisor. Once again, Mary's voice told me it was the right woman I needed to talk with. I found out she was Catholic and she was a beautiful Hispanic lady. At first I didn't want to talk to her because of the fear of rejection but little by little I began to share a story about my spiritual life and she seemed to understand. She would tell me that she was praying for me.

Then one day as I was walking down the hall on my way to a lunch break, I ran into an old friend. A thought ran through my mind. I remembered once reading in the company newsletter about this man's wife. She is a missionary and I believe she has traveled to Africa to help the poor. They have a son who is a pastor at a Christian church. My friend was a supervisor on the other side of the factory so it was very rare for the two of us to meet. As I glanced up and saw Doc's face, I heard Mary's voice tell me to go and speak with him. I asked if he had a spare minute. He said sure and we left the lunchroom and sat out on the patio away from other people. There I shared with him the unusual experience I was going through. He was so excited.

He said, "I am sorry but I am not able to quote the Bible verses, but I will tell you the stories that are coming to my mind."

This was very helpful for me. As time passed, I began to see how the stories he was telling me were matching the events I was going through. He even shared a story on how his wife had met of group of nuns in Africa who helped them when they encountered some problems while traveling overseas.

*Chapter Fifteen*

Meanwhile my life at home began to have major changes taking place. There were unforeseen events taking place in the house. Doors that were locked were standing open upon our return. Things were moved and hidden in the house. During this time, my husband and I were informed by the court system that we were not to contact our daughter or grandson. This did not stop me from praying; in fact it increased my prayer time. Mary's voice continued to keep me focused. Many times, she would assure me that they were being taken care of. I was not to worry. Yet the other voice continued to put fear and doubts in my mind.

At the same time, we were learning new things we had not noticed before. I felt like we were having a crash course. I had no clue as to why I needed to know these things.

Looking back to the events it seemed so educational but I had no reasonable answer as to why I had to go through the learning process. Simple things like filling a gas tank, reconnecting the hose to the pump after fueling, and hearing the three beeps. It was to represent the Father, the Son, and the Holy Spirit.

As we drove down the street, the licenses plates on the cars ahead of us became messages. As we looked at the letters, they became words that were spelled phonically. The numbers sometimes played an important part. This is when we first realized that we were being linked to the Bible. What we were seeing on the license plates became messages to us from the Lord. Through this procedure, I learned this was called the renewing of the mind.

As I slowed down and became more aware of my surroundings, I was being taught mentally the meanings of colors. Green was to remind me of the Garden of Eden. Blue for the color of dress that Mary wore. Yellow is for the Son of God, red is for the blood of Christ, and purple stood for royalty.

In Galatians 1:12 it reads, "For I neither received it of man, neither was I taught it, but by the revelation of Jesus Christ."

It was about that time I discovered the color of my car was no accident. It was in God's plan that I should drive a teal colored car. When the colors blue and green are combined, it makes teal; Blue for Mary in the green garden which is our world. It was brought to mind that every time I looked at my Saturn car, I should think of the planets that God had created at the beginning of time.

The voice of Mary also led me to start reading the Bible. I would open the Bible and scan a page and the verse would seem to jump right out at me. Most of the time it was only one or two verses. Then by the end of the week, I was told mentally to write the verses in a notebook. Then I would go back and read them and they just seemed to fall in order. It was unbelievable!

As I was dealing with all these new changes in my life another set of events began to unfold. I could not understand what was happening to me at the time. There would be times when walking through the house for some unknown reason my body would fall to the floor. I felt like I was pasted there, as I could not move a muscle. Since I could not move at all, all I did was pray and talk to Mary or our Lord. After a short time, I would get up and go about the things I was doing in the house such as dishes, as if nothing had happened. Each time this happened, I felt a great peace come over me. Later on I learned this is called resting in the spirit.

As the weeks passed by all these things continued to be part of my life; then came a new twist of events. I had gone to a Tupperware party, and when the order came in, we drove over to pick up the items that had arrived. As we were leaving, Mary spoke to me and told me to share my story with them. To my shock and disbelief, within a few days, they called and said Mary was speaking to the man of the house. In my mind, I could not understand why Mary would speak to a Methodist man. Yet he shared with me about hearing the voice and seeing the visions of Mary.

A few days later, a friend of the family had stopped over for a visit. Once again, I shared my story with this young lady. About a week later, I received a phone call. She was very excited and seemed extremely happy. I asked how she was doing. She said that she had just left college and was on her way over to her dorm. She said while she was driving she heard a voice talking to her. She said there was no one in the car. She had checked the back seat and no one was there. She knew it was Mary. She said that she had just driven past a statue of Mary when the voice began to speak to her.

Once again, I was confused for she also was not Catholic. She went to a Christian church. I was beginning to think that I was contagious. Another week went by and a young couple who my husband knew stopped by for a visit with the new baby. Once again, I was told to share my story. Sure enough, they called later to say Mary was speaking to the wife.

At this point in time, I began to feel a close connection with all of these people of a variety of ages. There were constant calls between all these families. Mary was directing us to come together on weekends for pot luck dinners.

As I watched these people grow in their faith, I could not believe the strong relationship they had developed toward our Blessed Lady. An unbelievable bond was taking place between the families. Later on I learned this is what is called a spiritual family. They too were struggling with hearing the other voice but we would call each other and help one another according to Mary's voice. There were times when they needed money or some other assistance. Mary would tell us how to help each other even before we would ask if they needed something.

I felt more at ease now because I found other people like myself. Yet in the back of my mind, I was wondering if this was not coming from Satan because of all the different denominations coming together.

After all I was raised at a time in history when people were supposed to date people of their own religion. It was frowned upon to visit another church of another religious background. I can remember when I was young, the nuns would tell us we would go to hell if we stepped foot into another denominations church. Yet, all of us were led to attend our individual churches of a variety of denominations.

## Chapter Sixteen

One weekend, Mary led us to take a short trip out of town to a small community named Strawberry. It is a beautiful little town and there she led us to go and see a one-room schoolhouse. Everything in the building was antique, right down to the old fashion desks that my old school had when I was very young.

As I toured the room looking at the old books, Mary spoke to me about the pioneers; their style of life and the practice of bartering. We also were led to an old-style restaurant. There was an old fireplace in the dining room with plants hanging everywhere. I felt like I had stepped back in time. At that time, Mary's voice told me I would be pioneering in my field. I had no clue as to what she meant but I had found that each day was now an adventure. I am sure it must have been the same for those people back in the pioneer days. I truly enjoyed my day out especially the big piece of homemade pie.

There were also different changes taking place in my life as Mary's voice began to change my life style. Grocery shopping was my major change. As I walked down the aisle, I was told what to put into my cart. If I picked up something, I was told it was not needed. By the time I had reached the checkout area, my basket had only a few items. My basket contained mainly fruit, vegetables along with a little red meat and fish. There were no desserts or snack food!

Next came the clothes; Mary's voice led me to purchase a long dress. It was dark in color with pink roses and a white collar. Definitely not my choice of dress; I was a baby-boomer with short skirts. I never wore the color pink, especially roses, but I purchased the dress and wore it to church.

I kept a close eye on the changes that were taking place. Our new friends, Bible reading, new healthier diet and a proper way of dressing surely this was not coming from Satan.

My husband and I decided to take a trip back home. The voice of Mary encouraged us to go. He had no doubts in his mind who was speaking to him. Anytime I rejected what was said, he would refer to me as the doubting Saint Thomas, which I greatly resented. He never grew up in a church. I was the one who attended Catholic Church, and yet I had a hard time accepting the fact that I was being spoken to. I was in denial and felt unworthy.

Although I must admit he told me when the speaking started, he could not understand where it was coming from. He said he searched the entire house looking for hidden microphones and speakers. I knew the voice went everywhere with me, in the factory, grocery store, mall and in the car!

*Chapter Seventeen*

We stayed with my friend and her family. I knew her since high school. There we spoke openly about what was happening to us. With the encouragement of the voice of Mary, we decided to go to Holy Hill. Holy Hill is the National Shrine of Mary Help of Christians, which has now been elevated and formally known as the Basilica of the National Shrine of Mary, Help of Christians. They say that as many as 500,000 people come each year, from all over the world to make their pilgrimages to worship, meditate or to pray for healing. There is also a monastery on Holy Hill where the Carmelite monks live.

Upon entering the shrine, I went off to the side chapel. I knew I was supposed to light a candle. The chapel was full of people. There in the front of the room, high in the air is a beautiful life-sized statue of Mary and Jesus, as a small child, standing next to her. Her eyes are looking downward. As I walked into the chapel I saw a Hispanic lady standing near the alter. She was crying and her eye makeup was running down her face. She was wandering around looking for a pew to sit in. I remember glancing up in her direction. I tried not to pay any attention to her because I had my own problems and that is why I was there. I took my seat in the front row. I started to mentally pray to Mary. I told her I was there for a sign of some sort because if I didn't get an answer over the weekend, I knew that I would have to go home and call a psychiatrist. No sooner did the thoughts run through my mind, than I received an answer. The voice told me to turn to the lady behind me. I glanced over my shoulder to see who was there and it was the Hispanic lady. She was kneeling down and praying. She was still crying. I looked back at the statue and mentally said to Mary that she will not even understand what I am saying as she is Hispanic. Once again, I heard in my thought waves, "Tell her what she is praying about will be taken care of."

I reached over and touched her hand. Then I said, "Whatever you are praying about, don't worry. It will be taken care of."

She looked at me and said, "What did you say?"

"Don't worry. You will get an answer."

Just then she stood up and looked at me, her arms went up in the air and she said, "Oh praise the Lord Jesus Christ."

Then she flipped backwards on the floor. As she fell, it sounded like a watermelon breaking on the floor. No one caught her. She just laid there. I remember sitting and looking around the room.

It seemed like everything just stopped. Nobody moved to help this lady. I could not even move to help her. I thought to myself why am I not moving? It seemed like a few minutes had passed, when an usher came in. He bent down and felt for a pulse in her neck.

Then he said to the man at his side, "She's fine." Then they both walked away.

At this time, Mary told me to go to the woman. I knelt down beside her and put the sign of the cross on her forehead. She did not move. I heard that I should do it again. Once again, I repeated the sign of the cross and then she began to move around. I helped her up off the floor. Then both of us went and knelt together. I put my arm around her and asked if she was all right. She shook her head "yes."

Then she said, "I have been so fearful, the Virgin Mary has been coming to me this last month. I see her and she speaks to me. All I can remember is having this feeling of being overjoyed in my heart."

I cannot express how I felt at that moment because here I was all the way from Arizona and came to Wisconsin, to kneel in this little chapel and had asked Mary to send me a sign and here was another woman praying for the very same thing.

I began to smile at her. I put my arm around her and I said, "I know how you feel."

She told me she did not feel worthy that Mary should speak to her. Lord, I could really understand this. I told her not to worry, for Mary was also coming to me. I told her that Mary comes and puts her face next to mine.

I said, "Do you know what I do? I mentally put my face against hers. Sometimes I give her a kiss on the cheek."

The lady smiled at me, then she said to me, "Do you believe that the Virgin Mary could come to people of all faiths, religions, and creeds?"

"Yes, I guess so."

I was thinking of a time long ago, when I heard of stories of the Virgin Mary appearing all over the world, and sometimes leaving a rose.

Then she asked me, "What is your name?"

I replied, "Nancy."

Then I asked, "What is yours?"

"In the United States, they call me Maria."

We gave each other a hug. Then I told her I had to leave to join the others for breakfast in the cafeteria. As I walked out of the doors,

I looked at the glass cases full of crutches and braces that were left behind from people who received a miracle there.

As I left the church I glanced up at the main alter, I saw two large beautiful pictures. I later learned that they were pictures of Saint Teresa of Avila and Saint John of the Cross. The church has the most stunning stained glass windows. The building is very large and the sounds of the organ echoes through the building. As I took the elevator down to the first floor, I watched the people as they were walking on the paths towards the area where there are life size statues of the Stations of the Cross.

I had finally caught up with my group. They were shopping in the gift store. Then we went to breakfast.

It was that morning after we left the church that I realized I was now hearing a male's voice speaking to me. I knew it was Jesus. Mary had taken me to her son and then she stepped back.

I told my husband what had happened to me and I said the voice of Jesus was telling me I needed to go back to a small church in

Newburg where I grew up. It was the church where I had my first Holy
Communion, Confirmation, and I was married there. I went to the
rectory and there I found a new priest. He was just on his way out the
door for a meeting.

He said, "I would be glad to give you the key so you could go in
and pray. When you are finished, just drop the key off at the convent
next door."

It was like a dream come true. I took the key and I went in to the
Sacristy. A Sacristy is a room where the priest keeps their vestments
and the other things that are used for church services. I had to find a
particular statue that I needed to see. I used to pray in front of this statue
when I was a small child. This statue is called the Pieta`. As a child, I
can remember praying there. When I was finished, I would stand on the
kneeler and stretch up on my toes to reach the nail holes in his extended
hand. I would kiss the nail hole and say a prayer that the nuns taught
us. "Forgive them for they do not know what they do."

I walked to the front alter and turned around and looked at the
pews, the Stations of the Cross hanging on the wall, beautiful stained
glass windows, and upon looking up, I saw the choir loft where I
once sang for many years as a young girl. The church looked exactly
as I remembered it. At the same time, it looked much smaller than I
remembered.

I walked to the back of the church only to find that the statue had
been removed and in its place, they had built a restroom. So I turned
around and walked back up to the alter and sat in the front pew and
looked at the other statue of Mary at the side alter. My thoughts went
back to a time when I was a little girl when I sat in this same pew talking
with mother Mary and wondered why her lips were not moving. Now
here I was as an adult sitting in the same pew and looking into the
eyes of the statue as my thoughts continued to speak to me. I was still
very disappointed at the thought that my favorite statue was no longer
there. I felt an emptiness inside of me.

It was getting late and my husband said it was time to leave. As I
stood in front of the alter the thought came to me to look back at the

big double doors in the rear of the church. Then I saw my favorite statue.

I remember shouting to my husband, "Wait! I see it!"

Then I ran down the steps and down the aisle as fast as I could. I went through the big double doors, around a corner to my right, and then turned left. There it was.

As I walked up to the statue, I saw Mary with tears in her eyes and tears falling upon her cheeks. I had to take a second look because I did not remember the tears being there. She holds her son in her arms after he was taken down off the cross on which he died. Her head is bowed in a downward position.

As I approached the statue, I put my finger into each of the nail holes and into his side; my tears began to flow.

I said, "Forgive them for they do not know what they do."

Here I was after all these years repeating the same actions I had done as a child except this time I did not have to stand on the kneeler to reach Jesus's hands. I bent down and kissed his hand.

The next thing I remember I was mentally reaching up, taking hold of the crown of thorns and breaking them apart. I could hear the cracking noises as I began to pull the thorns out of his head; I could feel the blood run down over my hands. I was sobbing and thinking how anyone could do this to my Jesus. Then I saw a white basin and a large white towel. I took a piece of cloth and began to wash his body. Then I wrapped a white sheet around him and held him in my arms just as Mary, his mother, had done.

I began to realize that Jesus was no longer suffering and I did not need a statue to connect with Him any longer. Through this process I could hear the Lord more clearly as we began a new journey together. He is alive, my risen savior Christ! Now I felt a sense of fulfillment. I came to understand why the Lord wanted me to return to the church where I grew up. I felt a sense of completion now; it was time to move on with my life.

*Chapter Eighteen*

After I returned home from my vacation, I was still thinking about finding my statue when I realized that it was impossible to see the statue from the front alter.

The Lord began to bring to my mind what I had seen, it was then I realized the only part of the statue I had seen was just the arm. It was from the elbow down and the hand was extended out toward me. It had the shiny surface just as if you were looking at the actual statue.

The more I thought about it, the more it bothered me for I knew it was impossible to see that statue from the front alter. I called my sister, Diane, and asked her to check it out for me. I also spoke to an aunt who still attends that church and I was told that the statue was moved to that area many years ago.

It now sits at the backside entrance of the church. Upon entering the church there are several stairs you climb and on the right side, stands my beautiful statue surrounded with flowers left behind by others who come to pray. I smiled to myself as I recalled walking up those same stairs as a child since we had to attend mass every day before school started.

It was through that event that the Lord was teaching me about visions. As time passed, my spiritual family began to hear the Lord's voice speak to them. Also, our visions and connection with Mary was also broken. All visions of Mary totally disappeared.

After the trip, I felt myself slip into a depression, which lasted for about six weeks. I knew why, I felt the loss of Mary. I was no longer hearing her voice to guide me. I missed seeing her face and feeling her check against mine, and the comfort I felt when she was close to me. It felt like a death had taken place.

Each time I wanted to pray the rosary I heard, "Not needed." I could not remember the words to the prayers. It was as if someone had erased them from my mind. Then the Lord spoke and said, "Not needed." Then the Lord spoke and said, "You can talk to me now."

The Lord began to teach me to walk in faith and to follow him. He was teaching me to battle Satan and I was afraid because I was walking in unknown territory. It seemed every time I would reach out to someone for help in this world, the doors were closed. I was learning more each day to rely on his voice and to walk in faith. I had to learn to follow directions. Later I learned this is called being obedient to the will of God.

The Lord taught me that we are connected or linked to one another. One day I heard the Lord say to call Patty. I shared with her all the things that were happening to me. Her response was unbelievable.

She said, "So what is the problem? You know that the nuns used to teach us that Mary would speak to us. I guess it is your time".

We had known each other since we were five years old and had gone to the same grade school for a while. Yet she seemed to understand what was happening. I felt comfortable after speaking to her.

Meanwhile, Jan and Earl, our Methodist family, had contacted their lady minister (whose name is Mary) and they spoke to her about what was happening to all of us. Then a group of people from the church came to their home and they discussed with them all the events that were taking place. We were told that we were receiving the gifts of the Holy Spirit! Something new! We were told that we were battling Satan because of our spiritual growth.

We also learned that the group of people who had come together was to be considered a spiritual family. I found this to be true. Jan and Earl were having financial problems because Earl had diabetes and needed medications, and their car was in need of repairs. They needed food, moral support, and lots of prayers. This was the reason why the Lord had put us together. The Lord led us to take money out of our retirement account and help them get through the crisis. The Lord was showing us that our money is not ours but his. Through his guidance, we were able to help this family.

Each day I would open my Bible and a verse seemed to stand out from the page. Then the Lord taught me how to journal. At first, it seemed like a waste of my time, but each day the Lord would bring to my mind that it was time to open my Bible and read. It seemed a veil had been lifted from my eyes. It was amazing how the Bible began to speak to me.

In Luke 1:45 it says, "And blessed is she that believed: for there shall be a performance of those things which were told her from the Lord." In Luke 10:23-24, I read, "And he turned him unto his disciples, and said privately, Blessed are the eyes which see the things that ye see: For I tell you, that many prophets and kings have desired to see those things which ye see, and have not seen them; and to hear those things which ye hear, and have not heard them."

As time passed I felt the need each day to pick up my Bible to read because I felt God was giving me a message each day.

It was also during this time when my husband and I attended a Sunday mass at Saint Vincent De Paul Catholic Church. I could not figure out why we had to go to a Spanish service. Neither one of us spoke Spanish, but the Lord was leading the way. The priest was a Caucasian male and to my surprise during the service, I understood one phrase of what he said. He repeated it several times. I heard him say, "Mary 9-1-1."

After the mass, the priest thanked us for coming.

I asked him, "What did you mean when you said, 'Mary 9-1-1'?"

He looked puzzled. Then he replied, "You do not speak Spanish?"

We replied, "No."

He smiled and then told us that they were selling the "Catechism of the Catholic Church."

I headed right to the bookstore and made my purchase. As I began to look through the book, my thoughts led me to read the chapter on prayer. This helped me feel more comfortable with my spiritual family of different denominations. In my mind, I kept questioning if this was truly coming from God, because years ago when I was growing up it was quite a different story. In fact, I remember hearing at one time that if we went to another church we surely would go to hell. As teenagers, we were encouraged to date people of our own faith. I also read that God tirelessly calls each of us to a mysterious encounter known as prayer. Then I began to think back to the many times I had problems over the years and how I searched for God's help. It never occurred to me to thank him for the end results.

Things always seemed to work out for the best. I knew God answered my prayers, but at the same time, I never realized that a relationship with our creator was possible. Yet the Bible is full of stories about men and women having a relationship with God.

*Chapter Nineteen*

Growing up Catholic, we were never encouraged to read the Bible. As I began to read the stories, I found that God dealt with each person differently but each person went through a test of faith.

I did not understand at the time what was happening to me but as time went on, I began to realize that God was seeking me. God began to put all the right people in my life to help me learn about a spiritual journey. I had no clue what a spiritual journey was or what happens to you as you begin a new life with Christ. Some people call this a born-again experience.

The Bible says in Luke 11:9, "And I say unto you, Ask, and it shall be given you; seek, and ye shall find; knock, and it shall be opened unto you." It was then that the Lord brought to my mind that during my time of prayer for my daughter I was praying from my heart. I spoke to him as if he were right next to me.

As my thoughts spoke to me, I was told that I was going down a path of spiritual enlightenment. To my surprise, I found this Bible verse, John 1:9 "That was the true Light, which lighteth every man that cometh into the world."

In the "Catechism of the Catholic Church," by Cardinal Joseph Ratzinger, I read about people who are led to pray for others, such as the nuns, monks, hermits, and prayer groups. In this book, I found information on Christian prayer. The author discussed many subjects including the gifts of the Holy Spirit and a word called discernment.

I have heard many people speak about discernment. What I realized is there are different ways for each individual for this process. Some say they feel it from the heart, others say they just know it. From my own experiences, I learned to mentally ask who is speaking. If I hear, "It is I," or "God," or "Jesus," I just keep asking until I hear, "It is I, Jesus Christ of Nazareth, the Nazarene." Then the Lord showed me a Bible verse in Matthew 2:23: "And he came and dwelt in a city called Nazareth: that it might be fulfilled which was spoken by the prophets, He shall be called a Nazarene."

Sometimes, I heard, "It is I, Satan."

Then the Lord taught me to say, "Get behind me Satan," from Mark 8:33, "But when he had turned about and looked on his disciples, he rebuked Peter, saying, Get thee behind me, Satan: for thou savourest not the things that be of God, but the things that be of men." Or "I rebuke you in the name of Jesus."

I learned to discern my thoughts by mentally picking them apart to see who was speaking to me and making sure, they lined up with what the Bible teaches us. In Romans 12:2 it reads, "And be not conformed to this world: but be ye transformed by the renewing of your mind, that ye may prove what is that good, and acceptable, and perfect, will of God."

There have been times when I would be praying about something and someone would come up to me and start talking about the subject I was praying about. Other times I would ask a close friend to pray to our Lord and ask something about my prayer and then the two of us would join in prayer and then the Lord would give us the same answer. He gave us different words but the same meaning. It was confirmation that the Lord was answering my prayer.

I also read about spiritual directors, something called a prayer corner, and they talked about pilgrimages. A spiritual director can be a pastor, nun, or another person who God chose for you to link up to as a prayer partner. A prayer corner means personal prayer. To me it is an ongoing communication with the Lord through my thought process. Pilgrimages are earthly journeys towards heaven. As time went on I found I was able to pray at any given moment night or day.

Now I had all this information but I still did not know exactly what God was trying to show me. In the past, I never attended classes at the church; I only went to Sunday services. Now the Lord was teaching me something new and it was not through a human's voice, but the thoughts that were going through my mind. It was connecting my real world with my spiritual world at the same time; they were blended together as one. What I learned later on was that God was giving me a glimpse of my future, of things to come and to learn when one searches for God.

The phrase, "the same but different," was constantly used to remind me that the real world and the spiritual one are going on at the same time. There is good and evil combined and that I had to learn to pick them apart and keep my mind focused on Jesus' voice and listen to his directions as I walked in the real world.

In Matthew 7:24-27, it says, "Therefore whosoever heareth these sayings of mine, and doeth them, I will liken him unto a wise man, which built his house upon a rock: And the rain descended, and the floods came, and the winds blew, and beat upon that house; and it fell not: for it was founded upon a rock. And every one that heareth these sayings of mine, and doeth them not, shall be likened unto a foolish man, which built his house upon the sand: And the rain descended, and the floods came, and the winds blew, and beat upon that house; and it fell: and great was the fall of it." As I learned to listen and follow, I felt I was being obedient to our Lord.

Sometimes I went through times of total confusion. Then the Lord taught me a new meaning for *discernment*. Then I found myself taking every thought captive. 2 Corinthians 10:5, "Casting down imaginations, and every high thing that exalteth itself against the knowledge of God, and bringing into captivity every thought to the obedience of Christ." I started picking apart my every thought. As I learned, I struggled to separate who was speaking to me. I broke down in tears many times.

The one thing that I did not understand was as I drew closer to God the more Satan attacked me. I felt like I was being pulled in two directions at the same time. I felt myself struggling, trying to make sense of what was happening around me. Finally, after a period of time I gave in and decided to walk in faith. Then through prayers and many tears, the Lord led me to a completely new way of thinking.

In the Bible, Isaiah 55:8 reads, "For my thoughts are not your thoughts, neither are your ways my ways, saith the LORD." The Lord was teaching me how to battle Satan in my mind and in the real world at the same time. I also learned during this time that only people who heard God in their own way could connect and understood each other.

# Chapter Twenty

I was led to make an appointment with my parish priest. I shared with him what was happening to me. I expected him to understand and at least pray with me. After our talk, I left in tears and felt humiliated. As time passed, I realized the Lord was breaking down the pedestal that I had for this priest. I did not know where to turn for help at this point in my life, so I decided to keep listening to the voice I recognized as Jesus.

The other problem I had was I really did not understand the term *spiritual director*. Nor did I know how to go about finding one. As time passed, the Lord led me to a prayer group. The meetings were held at night. At first, I was afraid to go out, but my confidence grew as I listened and was directed by the Lord.

It was a small group maybe fifteen people. They began their meetings with the singing of some hymns. The Lord told me to lift my hands up and I was shocked when one of the women in leadership came and told me I could not do that. I was expected to hold my paper with both hands. I remember feeling upset because I could not do what the Lord was telling me to do.

When I attended a second meeting, I was running late so when I arrived there were no more song sheets. So I lifted my hands while I sang and no one said anything to me.

Later on, I found this verse, 1 Timothy 2:8: "I will therefore that men pray everywhere, lifting up holy hands, without wrath and doubting."

Then I encountered another problem while the women were praying; I fell to the floor. This is what is called *resting in the spirit*. After I got up two women took me outside and told me I was never ever to do that again. They told me if I needed prayer, they would take me to a back room where only certain people were allowed to pray over others. I was shocked when they told me this and embarrassed by the thought. They were under the impression that I fell to the floor on purpose in front of a group of total strangers. Acts 10:10: ". . . he fell into a trance."

Since I was new to the experience of going to Bible studies or prayer groups, I did not realize at the time that when someone reads from the Bible it is a message from God to you. Through this experience of meeting new people, I met a man who was retired from the military and sometimes they would allow him to read the poetry he wrote. He said God told him what to write. They were beautiful poems.

Attending the prayer group only added to my frustrations. My only desire was to find a priest who could understand me and explain what was happening to me.

The visions continued and gave me a lot of peace. I think my most favorite was the Lord sitting at an old fashion wooden desk and there were lots of lighted candles sitting on it. He was bent over and writing in an old book with a feather pen and ink well. I could see it was my book of life. Sometimes I would try to look over his shoulder mentally to see what he had written but to my surprise, the page was blank. Then I would hear this soft-spoken voice say two words, "invisible ink." I would just smile to myself, for I learned that God has a sense of humor.

The other shocking encounter I had with the Lord was one day as I was working at my press. I felt an invisible face press up alongside of my face on the right side. I remember jumping right off my chair, and I almost ran to the rest room. As I calmed down, I mentally asked, "What is happening now?"

A soft voice spoke to me through my thoughts, and as I listened I heard, "I'm lonely!" I remember thinking, "What do you mean you're lonely?"

So I went back to work and found myself trying to mentally talk to God and yes, there were replies to my questions. After a time I felt like I was talking to an old friend. Psalms 27: 7-8: Hear, O LORD, when I cry with my voice: have mercy also upon me, and answer me. When thou saidst, Seek ye my face; my heart said unto thee, Thy face, LORD, will I seek."

I do believe the best vision God ever gave me (so far) was when one day as I was working a sudden picture came to my mind; I like to call this *my mind's eye.* This is similar to thinking of someone and picturing them in your mind. Except with the Lord, he puts the picture there for you to look at. In this particular vision, I saw a beautiful daisy. As I looked at it, all the petals fell off. All accept one! I remember giving a deep sigh. I wondered why God would do that. Just as that thought went through my brain. Another picture came to my mind. This time I saw a large magnifying glass held over the one single petal. I read three words that were written there. It said, "I love u." I just smiled to myself and thought, "Why the magnifying glass, Lord?" I heard two words, "bad eyes." I smiled and continued with my work. I realized that the Lord remembers every little detail.

Matthew 22:37 says, "Jesus said unto him, Thou shalt love the Lord thy God with all thy heart, and with all thy soul, and with all thy mind." Even though these visions continued on a daily basis, I still questioned if it was possible to have a relationship with God, who created the world.

Then I read 2 Corinthians 5:17-18. "Therefore if any man be in Christ, he is a new creature: old things are passed away; behold all things are become new. And all things are of God, who hath reconciled us to himself by Jesus Christ, and hath given to us the ministry of reconciliation." To be reconciled to me means I re-established my friendship with God that had been lost.

One thing I learned about visions was not all visions come from God! When my visions began with Mary, I had to learn to trust her. After I accepted the fact that she was coming to me each day, I would allow her to hug me. I even reached a point where I would kiss her on the cheek mentally. I felt comfortable knowing she was there to help and guide me through these unknown experiences I was having. One day as I was working, in my mind's eye, I looked up and saw Mary coming towards me. As I glanced up, I noticed her veil seemed to be draped across the face. This was not normal. As I watched her approach me, the veil fell open. I gasp at what I was seeing, panic hit me! I wanted to run, but I did not know where to go. I went into the bathroom, put my hands over my eyes and prayed. Of course, the other voices I was hearing was busy telling me that everything I was experiencing was from another planet. For the face I was looking at was the face of a space creature. It had very large eyes and no mouth!

For the next several days I lived in fear. I did not acknowledge the pictures that came into my mind. I tried to ignore the voice I was hearing. I felt like a small child when a parent scolds you and you completely focus on something else. After several days of this, my mind became very tired and I felt confused.

As time went on, I learned that not all visions come from God. I was struggling more now than any time in my life and I truly felt like I was losing my mind. My mind raced back to the first time I began to hear the audible voice calling me and the picture imagery that came to my mind and moved about freely as I watched it in living colors. I thought about how I was praying the rosary, and just a simple prayer asking God about my daughter had changed my whole life. I remember a prayer being said but I knew it was not from me and I knew it was coming from deep down from my heart.

As I listened, I heard a small voice say, "Please God take some of this abuse out of my life."

Then I felt like I was having a thought of my own for I was questioning if I had reached hell? Through trial and error, I learned Mary was fighting Satan. When she left and I received the visions of our Lord, the battling still continued. I felt like I had slipped into a whole new world and all my surroundings began to change to accommodate my new life.

In 2 Corinthians 3:16-17 it says, "Nevertheless when it shall turn to the Lord, the vail shall be taken away. Now the Lord is that Spirit: and where the Spirit of the Lord is, there is liberty."

Then in Luke 13:24 it reads, "Strive to enter in at the strait gate: for many, I say unto you, will seek to enter in, and shall not be able."

# Chapter Twenty-One

I knew whatever was happening to me was completely out of my control. I began to go through some unbelievable scenarios.

At first, it seemed like all the battles I was going though were in my mind. As time progressed, it also spilled into my everyday life in the real world. I kept having flashes of memories of the first day I heard the two voices speaking to me. I felt terrorized when I came home. My husband was gone at work and I was alone in the house. The first thing I did was to turn on all the appliances in the whole house, including the washer and dryer. I still could hear the voices. I went and sat on my bed and held the pillows over my ears, which was of no help.

Then I moved into the living room and I decided to write down what I was hearing. The visions of Mary were coming to my mind, and the soft-spoken voice reassured me that I would be taken care of. She was telling me to pray for the children. This particular sentence was repeated over and over again. As I wrote, the writings seemed to flow beautifully onto the paper. I was also hearing another voice and when I heard those words, I wanted to hold my pencil in the grip of my hand. I began to boldly print in large letters what I was hearing. To my shock, it was swear words. Words I knew I never used before. I remember getting down on my knees and crying out to God to help me. I was too afraid to tell anyone what was happening to me. My husband was working second shift and I was alone in the evenings. Even though all these things were happening to me, I knew God was taking care of me. At night, I struggled to get a few hours of sleep and went to work each day never missing a beat in my real world.

It was nearly six weeks later that my husband began to hear the voice of Mary as well. Then strange things began to happen in my house. Whenever I came home from work, I would find the front door standing wide open. It was very irritating to me that my husband would do this to me when he knew what I was going through.

I would wait up and explode at him. I was full of fear. Yet he said he remembered to lock the doors. The next day he installed a new lock on the front door.

Then strange things began to happen in my house that could not be explained. My husband had purchased for me a beautiful old fashion hairclip that had five hearts in the design. I had worn it several times and at the end of each day, I would remove it, lay it on the bookcase near the front door along with my wedding rings, and my watch so that it could be found easily each morning.

Then one morning the hairclip disappeared; I searched everywhere and it could not be found. Yet I remembered removing the clip and placing it on the bookcase the night before. After several weeks of searching, I found the clip in the desk area nicely hidden under a lot of papers. Also during this time, my wedding rings disappeared. Both of us tore the house apart and neither of us found the rings. Near the end of the week, I changed the sheets on my bed and when I pulled them off, I discovered my rings between the sheets of my bed. I was so happy to find them and I decided to put them and all my jewelry into a lock box at the bank.

Meanwhile, I was still hearing the voices speaking to me. One day I turned on the T.V. only to hear people arguing about how they wanted all the money and they wanted all the control of everything that existed. I could not figure out what they were talking about.

Then one day I went to get my hair cut. My husband picked me up and said there was this place I just needed to see and it was only a few blocks away. As we drove through the neighborhood, we came upon a house that had a large black wrought iron fence that surrounded their yard. On the fence was the initial M. The first thought that came to my mind was the name Mary.

My husband said to me that he was hearing that I needed to say a chant. I remember crying and yelling at him.

"I do not know any chants!"

Then all of a sudden a thought came to my mind. It was an old prayer that was said at the Latin masses. I prayed as I walked around my car and for some reason all the doors were standing open. I repeated the prayer several times.

Kyrie eleison, Christe eleison, Kyrie eleison. In English it means Lord have mercy, Christ have mercy, Lord have mercy. I felt overjoyed that I remembered these prayers from my childhood. At one time, I used to practice the Latin prayers with the boys who were studying to be Alter Boys, who served the priests at mass.

I had lost track of time. My days and nights began to run together. I found I had very little sleep. As I struggled from one event into another, I kept praying harder than I ever did before in my life. I began to talk to God as if he were standing in front of me. I could not understand what was happening to my mind. Yet I never seemed to miss a beat in my everyday life. I was still functioning as usual. I went through many scenarios that were not normal. I did not realize it at the time but I was fighting Satan head on but not understanding what was going on at the time. In fact, I was so stupid at that time that I never even put it together in in my mind that I was experiencing a spiritual journey.

It never occurred to me that many of the things that happened in my life all the way back to the age of seven were Satan's attacks against me. I could not remember anyone explaining to me just how Satan can work in someone's life or maybe I was just not listening or perhaps it was in God's timing that I was called forward to learn more about God through the Holy Spirit.

I knew that Lord was showing me the importance of Mary in my life. She was the one who guided me to her son and then stepped back and allowed me to form an intimate relationship with her son, Jesus. At the time, I did not know what was happening to me and I began to pray to our Blessed Mother out of fear of the unknown. Perhaps that is why the Lord led me to Holy Hill where the National Shrine of Mary, Help of Christians was put on my path.

The Lord also allowed me to meet a Carmelite monk and a priest who told me that I was one of those Charismatic people. It was then that I decided that whatever that was, I was not one of those people because of the tone in his voice when he spoke the word. I could tell it was not a good thing. The monk told me that I was highly gifted but I had no clue about what he was talking about.

The only thing I knew for sure was I felt like some door had been opened for me and I was walking down a narrow passageway. I was stepping out in blind faith! Calling out to God, as never before in my life, I felt as if I had died and had gone somewhere else. Everything seemed to look the same including the people except I felt a distance between myself, my husband, and even the children. I remember asking my husband several times if I had died and gone somewhere else. He kept repeating to me that it was me who had changed and not my surroundings.

It was a year later when I finely learned what a Charismatic person was and yes, I was one of those people! The Lord led me to a prayer group. It was there that I learned about the laying of hands. People from the group would lay their hands on someone then they would either pray in their own language or they would pray in the gift of tongues. Some people had the gift of prophecy, which was a message from the Lord. Sometimes people would read a passage from the Bible which to me it seemed like the Lord was speaking to me through the Bible verses.

I also found a pamphlet entitled "Understanding the Charismatic Movement," written by Rev. Msgr. Vincent M. Walsh. He also wrote a book entitled "A Key to Charismatic Renewal in the Catholic Church," published by Key of David Publications. They were of great value and well worth reading.

I knew I was fighting with every ounce of faith and strength in my body trying to hold on to my mind. I was not going to give up because I knew God was taking care of me. I did not know how, but I knew all things are possible with God. Mark 10:27 says, "And Jesus looking upon them saith, with men it is impossible, but not with God: for with God all things are possible."

One morning as I sat in church, I listened as Pastor Scott preached on waking the dead. He spoke on how we were to learn to guard our minds. That we should not just drift through life because we are being called to do God's mission here on earth. The choir sang a song called "Open the Eyes of My Heart, Lord." The pastor also spoke about things that are not always what they seem to be and that we are in a world at war and everyone has a crucial role to play.

The pastor spoke on how Satan wants to destroy you before you start your walk with God. For he knows you are being sent on a mission for God to touch other lives.

At the beginning of my spiritual journey, I went through several unbelievable stories. I think the hardest thing I dealt with was seeing my husband act so strangely. I knew it was not him. I had never learned that Satan could use people as vessels to come up against you. Looking back now, I can see that God was teaching me to separate the actions of the person from the person themselves.

I remember one morning when my husband invited me out for breakfast. I was so impressed as he never did this. He drove my car to the restaurant. Then he told me to leave all four-car doors standing wide open. I told him no, for I was worried that someone would steal my car. He insisted that his friends next door would be coming over to clean the car. I finally gave up and said to myself, "God, I need help." I followed him into the restaurant, sat down and ordered an egg and toast. I knew I could eat that fast. I sat very still crying and praying. Finally, the breakfast arrived. Then my husband reached over, picked up the saltshaker, and proceeded to pour a layer of salt over my food.

Then he said, "Eat little piggy, eat!"

At this point, I was really mad and began to cry harder. Then the waiter walked over to us.

He smiled at me then he put both of his hands up to his eyes like he was holding a camera, and said to me, "Smile pretty."

Then I refused to eat or drink anything. I had to sit and watch him eat his breakfast. When he finished we walked back to the car. He insisted that he would drive. I was so scared I felt that everything was out of control. To keep the peace, I let him drive my car. He kept telling me what a beautiful job they had done cleaning the car. In reality, it was filthy.

As he drove home, he was quiet. The problem was he only drove down the road about half a mile and turned into a driveway.

I asked him, "What are you doing?"

First, I thought maybe it was someone's house that he knew from work but then he smiled at me and said, "What is wrong with you? You can't recognize your own house?"

It was a small house with several antique cars sitting in the front yard. As we got out of the car and proceeded to walk to the back door, we argued the entire time. Thank God, there was a large black wrought iron gate over the back door. He got out his keys and I was crying hysterically by this time. I told him this is not our house and I was praying that no one would come to the door.

Then he laughed and said, "Can't you see that is our doorknob?"

I was shocked! It was the same style doorknob as our house except there was a small dent in it, which I quickly pointed out to him. He laughed again and agreed that if the key did not fit into the lock, I would drive the car home. He struggled with the keys and was quite upset with the fact that the key did not fit into the lock.

I held my breath and continued to pray the entire time. Finally, he consented to let me drive home. After we arrived home, everything seemed normal. He told me never to go back there again.

The next day when I came home from work, he had already left for his second shift job. As I walked up to the front door I saw it was standing wide open. I was so upset I could hardly control myself. As I sobbed, I got back into the car and drove straight over to the house that had the same doorknob but with a dent in it.

When I arrived, it seemed very quiet. I walked to the back door and knocked several times. As I stood there, I studied the knob and yes, it was exactly like the one at our house except for the dent at the bottom.

My tears were flowing and then I decided to leave as I walked back to the car, I noticed an old straw hat and an old empty whiskey bottle lying in the flowerbed. Then I thanked God that no one answered the door. At the same time, I was very mad at him for leaving the front door standing open.

Then I decided to drive back to the factory. I knew he would be sitting in the lunchroom having coffee and visiting with friends before starting time. When he saw me, I could tell by the look on his face that he was very irritated that I was there. We spoke to each other alone. I asked him if he was crazy leaving the front door open, when he knew what was happening to me. He swore that he had locked the door. He promised that he would install another new lock the next day. It was then that I told him I had gone back to that house and that upset him greatly. He made me promise I would never go back there again. When I went back home I searched through the whole house and all the closets and at the same time I could hear Mary's reassuring voice telling me not to worry and that no one was in the house. She reassured me that I would be all right.

A few days later, someone tried to break into a house near us. That evening, my husband insisted that we would sleep with our door wide open. Once again, I prayed for God to help me. It was about that time that I decided to call one of my daughters and let her know what was happening but I could not seem to get it out of my mouth. As we were talking, I heard her ask me if I still had the set of tarot cards. They were a birthday gift from a friend and they were sitting on a shelf for years.

I said, "Yes, but I can't remember how to lay them out."

Then she said, "I want you to get out the scissors and cut the black cloth into nine pieces and cut all the cards in half."

I did this as we were speaking. Later I carried them out to the trash can.

Months later when I saw my daughter in person, I thanked her for telling me to do that but she insisted it was not she who told me this information. She said I must have mixed her up with someone else. I was sure it was her.

All during this time, the voices and visions continued in my life. Often during the day, Mary spoke to me and sometimes during the night. Repeatedly she would say pray for the children. Yet at the same time, I knew I was fighting Satan. Many times Satan led me to believe that the voices I was hearing were coming from out space.

A movie I had seen as a teenager kept coming back to my mind; it was a story about a spacecraft that was moving people from earth to another planet. In the movie there was only one seat left so the man puts his wife in the craft and he decides to wait for the next load. After the door shuts, he walks up to the table, picks up a book, opens the cover, and reads. In the next scene he is screaming and pounding on the door trying to get her out. The book was entitled, "A Cook Book on How to Serve Man."

I became fearful at night alone in the house. This only encouraged me to pray even more, as I grew closer to Mary and prayed for strength. God was teaching me that not all visions come from God. I had to learn to separate the visions that were taking place. This was not an easy task but through prayer, I began to learn what God was teaching me. For I knew he was with me and carrying me as I drew closer to God. I became more dependent on Mary's voice as I felt peace even though I had to walk through the stories that were taking place in my life.

# Chapter Twenty-Two

I remember one Father's Day weekend many years ago at a time when I was very mentally drained from hearing the voices and seeing the visions. I was working long hours and had very little sleep. I cannot remember why, but at the time, my husband decided to throw all our pets outside. The dog was an indoor dog. All of our cats were declawed, so we never put them outdoors. I cried as I watched him walk through the house opening every curtain, entered the bathrooms, and threw the shower curtains up over the rods. Then he decided we should drive to Sedona. Meanwhile I managed to retrieve all the animals into the house. I kept reminding him that the kids would be calling today, because it was Father's Day, but he would not listen to a word I said.

I told him that I was driving. As I pulled out the driveway, I realized I had left my purse in the house and my wedding rings were not on my hand. I reached for my back pocket and felt my driver's license and I knew I had a credit card there too.

As I slid in behind the steering wheel of my car, the tears were running down my cheeks. I decided I would drive a few blocks then drive straight to the hospital.

No sooner had that thought run through my mind when I heard him say, "Don't get any funny ideas about taking me to the hospital."

I watched him slump down in his seat and as he spoke he sounded like a computer. It definitely was not him.

Then I asked, "Where am I going?"

"Sedona," was his reply.

As I entered the freeway, I felt panicked. I had never driven on a freeway before. Here I was passing semi-trucks and they were passing me.

After traveling for a few hours, we finally stopped at a rest area to use the restrooms. I was so happy to get out of the car. I walked over to a bench to sit down.

Then he told me, "Sit real still and do not move. A few of my friends are going to check the car for bugs; no matter what happens you are not to move."

The story of Lot came to my mind in Genesis 19:26, "but his wife looked back from behind him, and she became a pillar of salt."

My husband left me sitting alone. I just sobbed not knowing what else to do but pray.

As people walked by, no one seemed to pay any attention to me. The voice spoke to me and referred to the people as walking trees. Mark 8:24, "And he looked up, and said, I see men as trees, walking." Then I heard a horrible noise. It sounded like a semi-truck that was out of control. As I listened to the noise of the screaming brakes, I put my hands over my ears. The first thing I thought of was my car! I felt frozen to the seat, and I remembered whatever you do, do not move. As I sat there and cried I listened to my thoughts as they spoke to me. I was reminded that I had full coverage on my car and I was not to worry. I remember calling out to God for help. Then I realized there were no sounds of a crash. Suddenly once again, my husband was standing in front of me telling me it was time to leave.

I insisted again that I drive. He slid into the passenger's seat and once again, his voice sounded like a computer as he spoke to me. We finally reached the town and I pulled the car over to the side of the road. It was all that I could take! I could not go any further. I opened the car door, jumped out, and threw the keys to the ground. I wanted to jump off the embankment but he grabbed me.

"No!" he said. "You need to see the sunset. This is all for you!"

I tried to push him away; I did not want him to touch me. Then he said we should get a room for the night because it was getting late.

We found a motel nearby and checked in. Luckily I had a Visa card and driver's license in the back pocket of my jeans. There I stood. No purse. No wedding rings. No suitcases. The whole situation looked bad. Then he decided he was hungry and we needed to find a restaurant. My hope was restored. Maybe someone there could help me.

As we sat at a table in front of a window, he began to tell me that the people who were walking by looked just like other people we knew. Then finally, the waitress came over and took our order. He ate and I sat and watched him.

Then I made an excuse to go to the restroom. I pulled one of the waitresses over to the side and told her that my husband was acting very strange and asked her to please contact a policeman for me. As I watched her make the phone call, I prayed. I stayed in the restroom for a while. Later I peeked out the door and saw a cop sitting at the table with him. The waitress came over and gave me a hug and said everything's going to be all right.

The two men talked for quite a while. I sat at a table where they could not see me. I watched as the cop shook his hand and they said their goodbyes. I watched my husband continue to eat and the waitress showed the cop over to my table. He sat down, smiled at me, and said not to worry. He wanted to know where we were staying and he promised that he would check on me during the night. He said they had a good talk and that he was a little upset because only one of his children remembered Father's Day. He said he is more concerned over a large lump he has on his leg. I told him I did not know anything about this. The cop said goodnight and left. I went back to the table and he was just finishing his meal. He paid the bill. We walked back to the motel.

During all of this time, Mary's voice continually reassured me that everything was going to be all right. My fears were over powering me. I had nowhere to turn except to the Lord and pray as my tears continually flowed.

As we went to our room, I saw the motel manager.

She smiled at me and said, "No luggage?"

"No," I replied. "We left in a hurry and it is too late to drive home so we decided to stay over."

She gave me a silly smile and I thought to myself that she thinks I'm lying to her.

Once inside, he insisted that I shower first. When I was finished showering, he insisted that I sit on a chair and not move. It was finally time to go to sleep. It felt wonderful to lie down and not move.

He said, "We should stay awake all night."

In a few minutes, I drifted off to sleep then I heard someone talking. Then I realized it was my voice speaking. It confused me because I did not seem to be thinking about anything. Then I realized it was Mary using me to speak to my husband. I tried to move my body but I could not move a muscle. I was paralyzed. I listened as Mary spoke to my husband about different things I had gone through in my life.

Then something began to pull at my brain. Then all of a sudden, Mary began to talk about the birth of my last child. I wanted to scream but I could not move. My voice was not my own. My body began to have a seizure just like the same kind I had after the baby was born. At that time, there were two doctors present, but now only my husband was with me. I began to fear for my life. I mentally began to talk to God for help of any kind.

In Galatians 4:6, it reads, "And because ye are sons, God hath sent forth the Spirit of his Son into your heart's crying, Ab-ba, Father."

Just then, I heard my husband say that he understood. He asked if the seizures could be taken away. Then my body was still. I could feel all the muscles pulsating. I remember crying and then I fell back to sleep. When I awoke the next morning my husband showed me the very large lump on the side of his leg near his knee.

Mary's voice told me to get him to the doctor as soon as possible. We drove home and I unlocked the door expecting to see a large mess, but to my surprise, the house was spotless. All the animals were in the garage with the door closed. I knew when I left the cats were inside the house walking around the living room.

I immediately called the doctor and we went in the same day. They scheduled his outpatient surgery within a couple of days. We drove to Maryvale hospital and checked in. He was wearing a religious medal around his neck. He refused to remove it for surgery. I was told that the surgery would only be about an hour, or maybe two. As I sat and watched the clock it turned into several hours, finally a nurse called the waiting room. I was told that they were having problems. While removing the large cyst, his blood pressure dropped drastically. Luckily, a heart specialist was in the area at the time. The doctor later told us the cyst had grown down the side of the knee, but there was no damage to the kneecap. I seemed to heal in just a few days. It truly was a miracle.

Looking back to all these events that were taking place in my life I felt like Satan was out to destroy my mind. When I grew stronger in my faith, he attacked my real world.

*Chapter Twenty-Three*

In Psalms 14:2 it reads, "The Lord looked down from heaven upon the children of men, to see if there were any that did understand, and seek God." In Hebrews 2:4 it says, "God also bearing them witness, both with signs and wonders, and with divers miracles and gifts of the Holy Ghost, according to his own will?"

I have found my answer to my question where is God? God is everywhere!

In Acts 7:48-50 it reads, "Howbeit the most High dwelleth not in temples made with hands; as saith the prophet, Heaven is my thrown, and earth is my footstool: what house will ye build me? Saith the Lord: or what is the place of my rest? Hath not my hand made all these things?"

God has taught me to separate a person from the scenario they are going through and that sometimes a person can be used as a vessel to come up against you. Like the motel manager not to be too quick to judge others. Sometimes things are not what they appear to be.

I do hope you have learned something from my testimony or I should say my walk with God. I do believe the most important thing I have learned through this whole enlightenment experience is no matter what is happening around you, always keep your focus on God, and be open to the Holy Spirit. Be more aware of things going on around you, watch, listen, and follow God no matter how the circumstances look because he knows the outcome. Many times God has told me what to do but I questioned it. But after praying, I decided to do what

God was leading me to do. Sometimes I received immediate results and sometimes several months later, I realized it was the right decision. I thanked God because I could have made a bad choice for myself and for others around me.

I have learned many things about the spiritual life in the past years. The important thing everyone needs to do is to pray for the gifts of wisdom, knowledge, and discernment as well as to read your Bible daily.

My hope is to continue to share more stories with you on how God can use one life to touch so many other people when God decides to open the door. Many times the Lord refers to us as links or puzzle pieces. We are God's extensions, he can use us wherever we are needed, and many times in perfect timing, if we pray and listen he will guide you for what is needed at the right time.

There have been many times when I wanted to do more for someone but the Lord says, "No."

I have learned to be obedient to what God is telling me to do.

Unknowingly, God has moved me to a whole new level of prayer. It was something I never knew existed but was in the Catholic Church but for some reason never spoken about. God was putting me on a new path even though I felt unworthy. As time passed, I began to meet others like myself. The Lord has brought many priests, authors, evangelists from around the world, and pastors from Christian churches in order to educate me. He also gave me a spiritual director of his choice, Sister Elizabeth, a Catholic Nun. After a year and a half, she was removed from my life. She said I had out grown her. God also gave me a wonderful spiritual family of many denominations. One of the lessons I have learned is that God shows no partiality in a family of Christian people. God teaches them according to their level of understanding of faith in the Holy Spirit.

Over the years, my neighborhood has changed and most of my new neighbors are Hispanic families. I have had the privilege of praying with many of them.

The Lord has blessed me with a beautiful prayer partner. One I can really count on any hour of the day. Yes, she is the same but different. She is half-Irish and half-Hispanic. She is bilingual and helps me minister to people who speak only Spanish. The Lord has touched the life of my husband who is similar to me and understands my new life with God for he also walks with God now.

Also, the Lord has given me a good friend who is from another country, speaks Spanish, and completely understands my spiritual journey. Her mother was a leader of a prayer group in her country of Peru.

The Lord also gave me an extra son. He is just a little older than my own. He is a Hispanic man. Each morning he gives me a hug and I pray for him each day. With him, I also can discuss spiritual matters. His real mom went to heaven a few years ago. I pray that I am a good substitute for her.

Many years ago, I had a miscarriage. The doctor said he believed it was twins. I always felt in my heart that one was a girl and the other a boy. God has shown me that he has replaced the children I lost many times over.

The main part of my ministry has been at my factory. The Lord has led me to pray with people and help those in need. I help them through stressful situations, as I listen to the Lord as he guides me on what to tell them. At times, I go and pray with people's family members when they are dying.

I minister to people from all nationalities, but mainly to the Hispanic community. To me, they are all my brothers and sisters.

In 1 Corinthians 2:12-16 it reads, "Now we have received, not the spirit which is of God; that we might know the things that are freely given to us of God. Which things also we speak, not in the words which man's wisdom teacheth; comparing spiritual things with spiritual. But the natural man receiveth not the things of the Spirit of God: for they are foolishness unto him; neither can he know them, because they are spiritually discerned. But he that is spiritual judgeth all times, yet he himself is judged of no man. For who hath known the mind of the Lord, that he may instruct him? But we have the mind of Christ."

After my youngest child left home, God began to show me that he closed the door to my old life. Old friendships were broken.

I asked, "Why?"

The Lord said, "So that you would go and minister to the ones who need me."

"All my children moved away." Once again, I asked, "Why?"

"So your time would be spent serving me," he said.

Oh how true!

In my writings, I hope to share with you just how one life can make a difference when you listen to Christ.

I am very thankful to God for putting his mother into my life when I was a little child and allowing her to assist me in my spiritual walk with him. I love the way God constantly brings people into my life with the name Mary. Who would ever believe how God could reveal himself to me just because of a simple prayer that came from the heart. I asked God to help my daughter and he sent his mother to help me find him. This was just the beginning of my journey with Him!"

## Chapter Twenty-Four

Who would ever have dreamed that this door could open into a whole new world?

There is a very famous picture of Jesus standing by a door and he is knocking. One of my spiritual family members gave me this picture many years ago and it still hangs in my hall next to my bedroom door. There is something very special about this picture as you see Jesus knocking with one hand and in the other he's holding a staff like the shepherds use for their sheep. One day the Lord spoke to me and asked if I had seen anything unusual about the door in the picture. I replied that it looks like a regular door to me. Then he asked so where's the door knob? As I searched the picture I could not find one. I looked for similar pictures and sure enough not one had a door knob! The Lord showed me this verse in Revelations 3:20. "Behold, I stand at the door, and knock; if any man hear my voice, and open the door, I will come in to him, and will sup with him, and he with me."

Yes, it symbolized the personal relationship that had occurred in my life. As my relationship grew with him my real world changed. That door represented my mind. By listening and reading my Bible, I learned many new things about myself and I found a new path was opened to me. It was like being in a garden and walking through a very narrow gate. Allowing a voice I was hearing to guide my every step in the unfamiliar territory. I was now in. The directions were spoken to me through my thoughts sometimes audible and then there were times as if I were listening on a phone. It was my choice to follow the instructions and I believe I had made the right choice in the matter.

My choice was to go to Holy Hill in Wisconsin, and there is where I met Father Redemptus Short; a man that the Lord referred to as "Little Monk." I was also introduced to Father Gerard Taylor. He was the one that informed me that I was a Charismatic Catholic.

It took over a year for me to fully accept this title. But the Lord kept opening the doors to help me understand the process of learning about spiritual growth within the Catholic Church.

It was within this year that my friend, Nancy, and her daughter, Karen, heard about a prayer group at St. Frances Cabrini Church. She called and said I found some people who talk just like you! They went and spoke to the leader there, whose name was Jim. Later she contacted me and asked if I would come and meet these people and speak about the events that were taking place in my life. I was invited to be a guest speaker. I prayed and the Lord told me to go speak to this group of people. Arrangements were made and once again I traveled from Phoenix to Wisconsin.

I had asked my sister several times if she would please go and attend one of their prayer sessions but she never went. Instead she sent a co-worker named Ken. Being a L.P.N., the time never fit into her schedule. Upon my arrival to Wisconsin, I called my sister to let her know I was back on vacation and to my surprise she said, "You know what? I'm planning to go to that prayer group you are always talking about this week, because she also had time off. "Oh, my God!" It was then that I told her that I was the guest speaker that week.

It made me nervous to know that she would be there and also because I had never spoken in front of a group of people before. But the Lord told me everything's going to be all right. When that night came, Nancy and I drove to the church hall parking lot. As we were getting out of the car, I saw my sister arrive. Shock set in for she also invited my other sister and my three aunts! Ready or not God was giving me the opportunity to teach them about Charismatic Catholics.

Jim, I found out, knew my husband from many years before because they had both been in the Army National Guard together.

It was Jim who later invited me to travel with this prayer group to other states to attend National Catholic Charismatic Renewal Conferences, which until this time, I had never heard of before. In June of 1998, we went to the Franciscan University in Steubenville, Ohio. What an experience! There I heard Bishop Sam Jacobs, Fr. Michael Scanlan, Fr. John Bertolucci, Ralph Martin, Arlene Apone, Babsie Bleasdell, and Sister Nancy Keller . . . just to name a few of the guest speakers. The theme for that year's conference was called, "In the Name of the Father." They were preparing for the Great Jubilee Year of 2000. It was a wonderful event as each speaker had a workshop (a small class) and there they taught about different subjects relating to the Holy Spirit. They spoke on the Holy Spirit being the source of power for the Christian life and for the new evangelization which is repeatedly called for by Pope John Paul II. Over the years, I was given other opportunities to travel to other states like Pennsylvania and Texas to learn and meet other people who spoke about their encounters with God.

In one of my pamphlets from March 1997, Entitled a "Grace for the New Springtime," was an article about Mary being the mother of the church and how she was overshadowed by the Holy Spirit. She really was my gateway, what was so surprising to me was that they were celebrating their thirtieth anniversary of the Catholic Charismatic Renewal. At some of the conferences, I met several speakers who sold their books with stories of their encounters with God. Here are just of few of them: Sister Francis Claire, Linda Schubert, Babsie Bleasdell and Elisabeth Elliot. Over the years I have learned a lot from hearing these people speak and reading their books.

I thank God for my friends, Nancy and Karen, who connected me to this prayer group, and because of them, I learned about the Charismatic Renewal Conferences. The Lord refers to these events as a linking process that needed to take place in my life. As of this writing, it has been about nineteen years since my spiritual journey began. Looking back over those early years, I can now see how my life was split in two, but still blended together.

The first half of my life was done my way making all my own decisions with some mistakes. Believing in God but there really was no connections with God, just going through the motions that I was taught from a small child on. I would call it a religious way of life. I can look back now and see how God carried me through many situations but the interesting part is that I never seen how the devil played an active part in my life. The awareness of everyday stress was never connected with the evil side. I thought I was in control of everything. I was never fully aware of all the events that had taken place over the years were actually pieces of a large puzzle that the Lord had designed for me; some refer to this as "your journey in life." I was never taught that phrase nor had I ever really paid attention to setting a goal for myself, nor had I ever had visions or heard God speak to me during this time.

As for my second half of my life I became in tuned to my surroundings the challenges and distractions that were taking place in my everyday life. I became aware of a battle for my soul. I learned about the different levels of spiritual growth and that we are links to one another and puzzle pieces that can complete our journey in stages of spiritual growth. Our spiritual growth is a process that has to be taught to us in stages. Psalms 37:23, "The steps of a good man are ordered by the Lord: and he delighteth in his way."

I found myself wanting to please God all the time. By reading the Bible it gave me strength because it spoke of people who received visions and people in the stories actually sought daily guidance from the Holy Spirit. I learned that this is normal for a Christian's life. Proverbs 3:5-6, "Trust in the Lord with all thine heart; and lean not unto thine own understanding. In all thy ways acknowledge him, and he shall direct thy paths."

1 Thessalonians 5:19, "Quench not the spirit." As I read the Bible it became a learning lesson for me as the stories unfolded I became more aware of the relationship between Jesus and God, the Father. What I realized was that there can be communication between a human being and our creator. These examples made me aware of a living and invisible God who actually can participate in our lives and by listening we can make correct choices for ourselves and others around us; one of peace and hope for a better future.

There are definitely two worlds that are battling each other. In my early stages of hearing God's voice I was led to attend a church service at a Pentecostal Church. It was there that I met Pastor Coleman and his wife, Mary. They were from Cathedral of the Valley in Escondido, California. Their son, Joel, was the pastor at Faith Chapel. When I went that day they were announcing a weeklong series of lectures on a book entitled, "The Weapons of Our Warfare," written by Coleman and Mary Phillips. In one of the chapters he spoke on spiritual warriors. A spiritual warrior is a person who learns to stick it out, hang in there, and keep the ultimate goal of invading and defeating the enemy foremost in his mind. The enemy is the devil. Since the Lord told me I was a warrior, it helped to explain my purpose on this spiritual journey.

Later on, the Holy Spirit led me to attend Victory Assembly of God Church where I met Pastor Leroy Owens. I remember the first time I met this man in his office. I told him I was Catholic and I was having a problem understanding what was happening to me. He smiled and gave me a hug and said, "I love Catholic people, they have the strongest foundation of faith I have ever seen." He told me that I was led there to learn about rivals.

The Holy Spirit has led me to many people who have taught me about the spiritual life sometimes in person, through books and tapes. I have learned that God has a plan for each of us, some refer to this as discovering our destinies. 1 Corinthians 12: 4-11, "Now there are the diversities of gifts, but the same Spirit. And there are differences of administrations, but the same Lord. And there are diversities of operations, but it is the same God which worketh all in all. But the manifestation of the Spirit is given to every man to profit withal. For to one is given by the Spirit the word of wisdom; to another the word of knowledge by the same Spirit; to another faith by the same Spirit; to another the gifts of healing by the same Spirit; to another the working of miracles; to another prophesy; to another discerning of spirits; to another diverse kinds of tongues; to another the interpretation of tongues; but all these worketh the one and the self same Spirit, dividing to every man severally as he will. For as the body is one, and hath many members, and all the members of the one body, being many, are one body: so also is Christ." We all have talents and gifts that are given to us. There is a lot of material to help you learn about your journey, here are some of my favorites that the Lord led me to read: *The Practice of the Presence of God* by Brother Lawrence; *Mother Angelica* by Raymond Arroyo; *Safe in the Shepherd's Arms* by Max Lucado; *Good Morning Holy Spirit* by Benny Hinn; *Experiencing God* by Henry T. Blackaby and Claude V. King; *The Life You're Fighting For* by James and Betty Robinson. Another is Joyce Meyers who wrote a book entitled the *Battlefield of the Mind* which I highly recommend to all of you to read, as well as *When the Enemy Strikes* by Charles F. Stanley and *A God You Can Talk To* by Jesse Duplantis.

In fact just a few weeks ago on June 12, 2012, the Lord brought to mind that I needed to go to my Family Christian Book Store on 99ᵗʰ Avenue. So I went there and met an author who was having a book signing event. The paper he handed out said to read Jeremiah 29:11. "For I know the thoughts that I think toward you, saith the

Lord, thoughts of peace, and not of evil, to give you an expected end."
As the author, Mornay Johnson, shook my hand and asked my name,
I got the impression that he was a very friendly man. I only gave my
first name. He knew nothing about me. Then he proceeded to give
me a prophetic and destiny word for me from the Lord. He said I was
pioneering in my field. It was something the Lord told me many years
ago. He told me, "You are a forerunner for Catholicism." I purchased
the book, *Godly Success Unlocking the Door of Prosperity in Your Life*,
like the Lord told me to do. I highly recommend this reading material.
I laughed to myself as I looked at the picture on the front cover of
this book. It's a picture of a lock on a door with an old fashioned key
inserted into the lock. Through the keyhole a bright light is shining
through it. Yes, it is the light of Christ. Just as I began this chapter, the
Lord was showing me a picture of a door with no lock but through all
this information I have shared with you it is a key for an opportunity
to find, unlock and open your mind and heart to God. The subject has
come full circle "the door."

I would like to share with you one more story about the Lord
with you. One day the Lord asked me "What does the word Catholic
mean?" My reply was what do you mean Catholic means Catholic!
"No," he said, "Let's get out the dictionary and see what it means."
After a lot of complaining under my breath I found the dictionary.
It said, "Universal, general, all inclusive, comprehensive in interest,
sympathies or the like liberal (Webster's Dictionary, 1913)."

I love that word, "universal" for I have learned the teachings and
the works of the Holy Spirit were the same in each church the Lord led
me to. What I have also observed is there are many Christians still on
the treadmill in their lives. The Lord refers to them as "lazy Christians"
living in their comfort zones. Not willing to step out of the box and
move forward. Many of them cannot or will not let go of their past
sins, after all God forgives and wants us to move forward so he can use
us as vessels to do "His" work.

The church I now attend is Christian within a small Hispanic
community. There is one particular family that I'm very close to. Manuel

and his wife, Mireya, and their two sons come from a Catholic family in Mexico. They struggle here week to week, but over the years they have learned to pray, read the Bible, and rely on God. I have watched as the Holy Spirit has taken care of them spiritually and financially. Manuel's greatest desire of his heart is for his whole family to learn about Charismatic Catholics so they also can have a living relationship with God, our creator, and be led by the Holy Spirit.

There is another man that God has placed in my life that attends this church, his name is Francisco. Whenever I am led to pray over someone, he stands behind the person and is also praying. Sometimes the person rests in the Spirit. He catches them and lays them on the floor. I know he is very close to God.

Since I do not speak Spanish I have a translator who is the son of a pastor from Mexico. Pastor Ruben and his wife, Rosa Maria, not only raised two sons of their own, but also took in other children to raise in a Godly way. This family has given me a lot of spiritual strength over the years. God has given me the opportunity to watch Eliel grow from a teenager into a spiritually young man who is studying to become a future pastor. Sometimes he translates for the entire church and then there are times he just translates for me. I know that he is a special gift from God; he is just like a son to me, a spiritual family member.

Just yesterday as we were speaking by phone, he was telling me how he heard a pastor speak on why it is so hard for people to give their lives over to Christ. It's because when a baby comes into the world, we care for them and we teach it everything we know then at a certain point we teach them how to stand on their own and make their own decisions. But when we come into a fellowship with God, we have to turn <u>our whole life over to "Him."</u> Let <u>God make the choices for us.</u>

Then I heard him laugh and said that's the hard part, Nancy. I have to agree with Eliel, but I have learned God knows whats ahead of us on our path and the Holy Spirit can be our road block to a more peaceful way of living through making the right choices if we listen and obey. Will the Devil leave us alone now that we are walking with God? Of course not, because he has always wanted us to fail.

As Eliel said turn your life over to God, break away from your past, move forward, listen and follow God. Take the time and money He has given you and become his hands and feet. Use your life to serve Him.

Just remember the son died on the cross, he came into our world to teach us how to connect with the spiritual side of our life in a relationship with our heavenly Father. He came to serve man. He left and sent the Holy Spirit to guide us so we could pattern our life after him so we can serve each other with the love of Christ.

My message to you: do not be afraid of the unknown. The Lord is beside you at all times. He will guide you and teach you what you need to learn. Keep your focus on God at all times. Pray and learn to discern everything. God really has a plan for your life. Many of the people I spoke to over the years are those who don't attend a church, but my desire is to touch as many as possible and talk to them about God. Luke 8:11-15, "Now the parable is this: The seed is the word of God. Those by the way side are they that hear; then cometh the devil, and taketh away the word out of their hearts, lest they should believe and be saved. They on the rock are they, which, when they hear, receive the word with joy; and these have no root, which for a while believe, and in time of temptation fall away. And that which fell among thorns are they, which, when they have heard, go forth, and are choked with cares and riches and pleasures of this life, and bring no fruit to perfection. But that on the good ground are they, which in an honest and good heart, having heard the word, keep it, and bring forth fruit with patience." It's the planting of the seeds in the Garden.

# References

Holy Bible, King James Version.
Webster's Dictionary (1913). Word search: "catholic."